201 ESSENTIAL INTERNET TIPS

Over 250 pages of help for beginners...

- *Choosing the best service provider*
- *Connecting easily and quickly*
- *Sending and receiving email*
- *Visiting Web sites*
- *Enjoying newsgroups*

Published by Paragon Publishing Ltd
Paragon House
St Peter's Rd
Bournemouth BH1 2JS
Tel: 01202 299900
Fax: 01202 299955
http://www.paragon.co.uk

Managing Editor: Geoff Harris
Contributors: Steve Hill, Paul Douglas, Steve Patient, Clive Parker, Rowan Youlgreave
Layout: Jane Evans
Printed by: Caledonian International Book Manufacturing Ltd, Westerhill Road, Bishopbriggs, Glasgow G64 2QR
Published by: Paragon Publishing Ltd

Introduction

Does the thought of getting online intimidate you? Well join the club, because while many people in the UK are excited by the Internet's infinite possibilities they are put off by the technology involved. The Internet has acquired a reputation for being fiddly, frustrating and mired in arcane techno-jargon. This is a real shame. There's no need to worry about getting on the Net, as these days, getting a Windows PC or an Apple Macintosh connected to the Internet is much easier than it was just a couple of years ago. But things can still be confusing if you are not used to installing software on your computer, or if you are new to using computers in general. The thing to remember is that setting up Internet software isn't actually any different than setting up any other kind of program, whether it's a word processor, spreadsheet or game.

About this book

This book is written to help all beginners. It is crammed with 201 tips that cover the main areas of concern to new users – choosing the right service provider, connecting to the Net for the first time, using email, visiting Web sites and making a Web site yourself. Readers who have been online for a little while can also benefit from this book, since it contains lots of tips to help you use the Net more efficiently. And if you are using the Net more efficiently that means that you'll be saving money on your phone bill. Great news for you – bad news for BT!

Contents

Chapter One: Getting Connected to the Net 5

Chapter Two: Email 69

Chapter Three: The World Wide Web 101

Chapter Four: Newsgroups 165

Chapter Five: Making a Web Site 187

Glossary: All the Net jargon translated into English 221

Subscribe 254

CHAPTER ONE

GETTING CONNECTED TO THE NET

*What do you need to get on the Net – and how to
sort out the most common connection problems*

1

Buying a Net computer

Getting on the Net is actually quite cheap. Certainly, you don't need to go and blow £1500 on a top of the range, Pentium III dream machine just to send email and visit Web sites. That would be like using a bazooka to kill a fly. It's perfectly possible to get online with a 486 PC or slower Pentium, hooked up to a 28.8kbps modem. You can pick this little lot up for £300 if you look in the classified ads of magazines like PC Mart or Computer Shopper.

2

Minimum PC specifications

You'll need a beefy machine to run Windows 95 or
98. We recommend at least a 166MHz Pentium box
with 16Mb of memory, 32Mb if possible. The
smallest hard drive you should consider is 2Gb, since
files downloaded from the Net soon eat up storage
space. Don't forget that your Web browser stores
Web sites you visit in a special 'cache' of temporary
files on your hard drive: if you decide to use the
Internet Explorer and Netscape Navigator browsers,
you'll have two separate caches. An SVGA monitor
running at a minimum of 256 colours at 800x600 is
an absolute must.

3

The new PowerMac G3

iMac

PowerBook G3

Minimum Mac specifications

Macintosh users need at least a Motorola 68040 processor and 16Mb of memory. Again, 32Mb is recommended, if only because of memory-hungry Internet applications such as the Internet Explorer 4 Web browser. Get a good-sized hard drive, at least 2Gb, and a 13-inch or bigger colour monitor running at 800x600 in 256 colours. Note that you can get one of the sexy iMacs ("I" stands for Internet) for about £700 if you shop around or buy mail order. These make getting on the Net via easy – several Internet accounts are pre-installed on the machine.

4

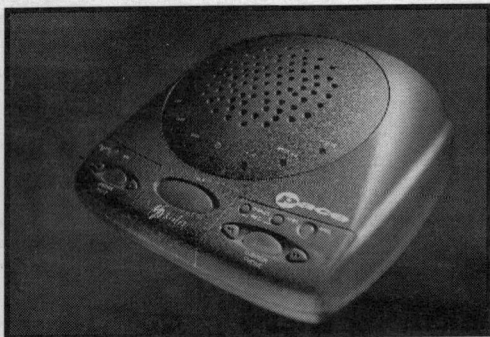

Buying a modem

While you don't need a top of the range PC, we
advise buying the fastest modem you can afford.
One hundred pounds should buy you a 56kbps V.90
modem suitable for your computer, which is 'flash
upgradeable' (this means you can easily upgrade it
to future industry standards). Buy from a reputable
name, such as 3Com US Robotics, Pace, Diamond,
MultiTech, Premier or Hayes, and make sure there is
a UK help line you can call at reasonable rates. If
you are buying a new Pentium-class PC, make sure it
comes with a fast internal modem – standard issue
these days.

5

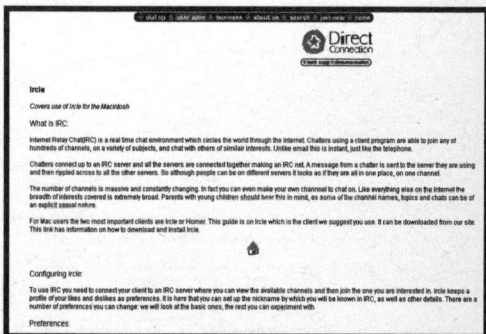

Choosing the right Internet service

Picking a suitable service provider is a big decision. Apart from the fact that home users won't get on the Net without signing up with a service provider, choosing an unsuitable or unreliable one can sour the whole experience of going online. It's important that you choose an ISP which offers installation software for your kind of computer, whether it's a Mac or PC. This is particularly important if you own a Mac – ensure that the technical support people are able to sort out Mac-related problems.

6

4. What are the telephone numbers?

Callers in the UK

We use three independent suppliers of telephone service in the UK. This gives our customers protection against failure of any single supplier.

Customers should choose from the numbers listed according to the type of equipment they are using. Calls to the wrong type of number might not work and may still be charged.

Call type	Green	Purple	Red	Orange
Analogue up to 33.6kbit	0845 212 0666	0845 212 1666	0845 079 0666	
V.90	0845 212 0666	0845 212 1666	0845 079 0666	
K56flex		0845 212 1666	0845 079 0666	
X2	0845 212 0666			
ISDN	0845 212 0667		0845 079 0667	
Orange data (multidigital)				0973 100666
Orange data (multianalogue)	0845 212 0666	0845 212 1666	0845 079 0666	

- K56flex and X2 are not supported services
- Orange analogue calls may be slower than digital

0845 numbers are described by Oftel as 'local call rate', and BT charges them at local rate. Other telephone companies might have special rates; contact your telephone company for their pricing structure.
The Orange number is charged by Orange at its standard Orange-to-Orange rate.

There are still a number of geographical number giving access to the Red HOME?, however unless you have some specific reason to use these numbers we do not recommend their use.

Callers in the Netherlands

For both analogue modems and ISDN calls, find the area you're calling from in the first table below, and then determine the corresponding access numbers from the second table below.

010	A1	0252	B3 F3	0475	F6	0547	F4
0111	A2 A4	0255	B3	0478	F6	0548	D3
0113	A2	026	D5 E4	0481	B4 E5	055	B5 E4
0114	A2	0294	C5 O1	0485	E4	0561	I12
0115	A2	0297	B3 O1	0486	B4	0562	B6
0117	A2	0299	B2 O1	0497	B4 O4	0566	I12 B6
0118	A2	030	C1	0488	E4 B5 O4	0570	E5

Keep it local

Check that the service provider lets you connect to the Net at local phone-call rates. Almost all of the larger companies now offer 'virtual' PoPs (points of presence). This means your modem can dial in using an 0645 or 0845 number to keep your phone bill down. Alternatively, there may be a local company that just services your town or city – check the phone book. Recently, the X-Stream Network (http://www.x-stream.com) has started to offer free Net access and free phone calls. If this is a success, expect others to follow suit.

Try a free provider first

With so many companies now offering free Internet access, you should try these first before signing away £10 a month to a subscription-based service. If you want to try out Dixons' Freeserve, simply pop into a local Dixons, Currys or PC World and pick up an installation disc. If you want to try out Virgin Net or LineOne (also free) get their contact details from the ISP listings in the magazine and get them to send you a disc. Remember that there's no such thing as the 'perfect' service provider that's right for everyone. Try a few out.

8

Watch out for help line charges

The catch with free service providers is that they charge premium rates for technical support via telephone. Most are now charging 50p a minute, including the big players such as Freeserve and TescoNet. Watch out for Arsenal FC and Breathe, which were charging £1 per minute when we went to press. Virgin Net is also charging a quid a minute, but you can sign up for a "customer care" package for £5.99 a month. You will have to pay this monthly charge whether you call the help line or not, so it's like an insurance policy.

9

ClaraNET exit

Joining ClaraNET

Which account would you like?

All new customers are eligible for one month's **FREE** trial with unlimited access time, whichever package you choose. Please note that this only applies to those customers who are opening a ClaraNET account for the first time.

If you decide to continue your subscription after your free trial, you will be billed at the start of your second month, based on the package you have selected. If you decide not to continue, all you need to do is notify us in writing before the end of your trial month. Include your <u>username and postal address</u> and you will have nothing to pay. If you do not notify us, the account will continue to run and you will be billed.

Please select the type of account by choosing one of the following options:

○ **Premium access**
  Annual: £99 + VAT Pay for 10 months' internet access and get an extra two months FREE. Unlimited access, no hourly charges. Includes 25Mb free webspace and full e-mail and newsgroup access. Payable in advance by cheque, Mastercard, VISA, Switch or Delta.

⊙ **Monthly: £9.90 + VAT** per month, unlimited access, no hourly charges. Includes 25Mb free webspace and full e-mail and newsgroup access. Payable monthly or quarterly in advance by Mastercard, VISA, Switch or Delta.

○ **Standard access: £7.65 + VAT** per month, Unlimited access, no hourly charges. Includes 10mb free webspace and full e-mail and newsgroup access. Payable monthly in advance by Mastercard, VISA, Switch or Delta.

Be careful with credit cards

If you're not impressed by the free ISPs and prefer to use a conventional one, such as AOL, make sure you get a free trial first. The only drawback with this is that you have to give your credit/debit card details when you apply for the trial account. If you don't want the account once the trial period ends, make sure you inform the company (preferably by email or letter) or you could end up getting charged for something you don't use.

10

Get the right deal for business

When choosing a service provider, it's good to have some idea of the kind of Net connection package you are looking for. If you want to use the Net for business – perhaps to set up a corporate Web site – you should choose a very reliable ISP that provides specialist support, so try UUNET (0500 474739) or PSINet (01223 577167).

11

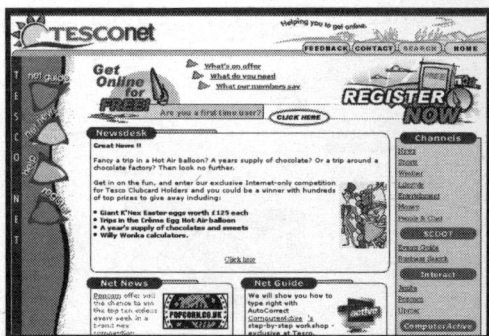

Get the right deal for home use

If you're just using the Net just for fun or stay in touch with family, then you should be fine with a free ISP such as Freeserve, X-Stream Network, TescoNet, LineOne or Virgin Net. Just remember that most free ISPs charge you extra for using the help line – calling up Freeserve's technical support costs 50p a minute, for instance.

12

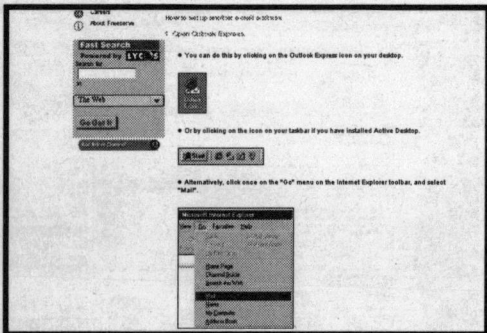

Multiple email addresses

Email is an important consideration when choosing an ISP. If the account is just for you, then you could settle for a company that offers a single email address. If the account is going to be shared by the rest of your family, then choose a free service provider that offers multiple email addresses, such as Freeserve, or a subscription-based provider such as AOL. This allows you to set up individual 'mailboxes' for each member of your family.

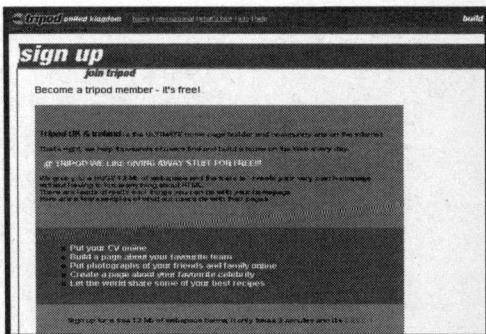

Reckon on the Web

Do you think you'll want to create your own Web page? If so – it's pretty easy – then you should choose a service provider that offers free Web space. Although you can squeeze lots of text-only pages into one or two megabytes of space, the room will soon run out when you start to add pictures. Most service providers now offer up to 15Mb of space, including free ISPs, while Easynet (0541 594321) offers an unlimited amount. If you are with an ISP and need extra Web space, you get it for free from these Web sites: Tripod (http://www.tripod.co.uk), GeoCities (http://www.geocities.com) or Fortune City (http://www.fortunecity.com).

14

Web for business

If you're running a small business and you want to
start a Web site, you will need an ISP that allows you
to use your Web space for business purposes – some
of the free ISPs do not permit this. If an ISP does
allow Web space to be used for business, you must
check if there are restrictions on the amount of
traffic it allows. Demon (0181 3711234), Force 9
(0800 0737800) and U-Net (01925 484444) are good
choices for the small business user looking to start a
Web site, but phone around.

15

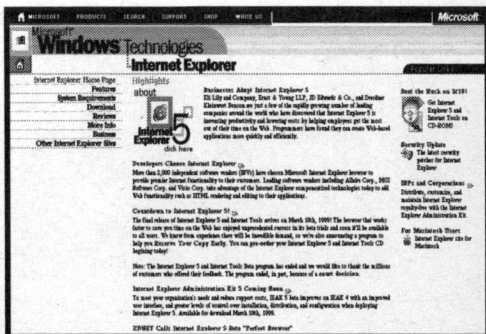

Signing up to an ISP

Setting up an Internet connection used to be a
fiddly and frustrating job. Thankfully, it's now a
simple matter of running a set-up program on a CD-
ROM or floppy disk, and everything is done for you.
Most ISPs now base their installation software on
Microsoft's Internet Explorer Web browser suite, as it
includes programs for all the essential Internet
functions – visiting Web sites, sending email,
contributing to newsgroups and making a Web site
yourself. Over the next few pages, we're going to
walk you through an ISP installation, using the
massively popular Freeserve as an example.

16

Welcome To Freeserve

free

| Install | Help | Cancel |

Freeserve – insert the CD-ROM

Insert the CD and wait for it to autorun. If it doesn't autorun, you will need go to the Start menu and select 'Run,' then type D:\install.exe and click the 'OK' button (assuming your CD-ROM is drive D and not some other letter of the alphabet). Click 'Install.'

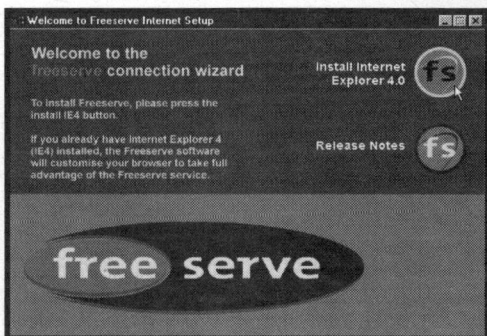

Freeserve – installing Internet Explorer (IE4)

You have a choice of installing the Freeserve version of the Internet Explorer 4 Web browser or reading the release note. If you haven't used the Internet before it's a good idea to read the notes as they give some important information on how you can (or cannot) use the program. Click on the 'Install IE 4' button to continue.

18

Freeserve Internet Explorer Setup

fs

Internet Explorer 4.01 SP1

Welcome to the Internet Explorer 4.01 SP1 Active Setup wizard, which will guide you through the process of installing Internet Explorer.

Note: Internet Explorer 4.01 SP1 replaces previous versions of Internet Explorer.

Product ID: 71929-OEM-2000014-12345

freeserve

< Back   Next >   Cancel   Help

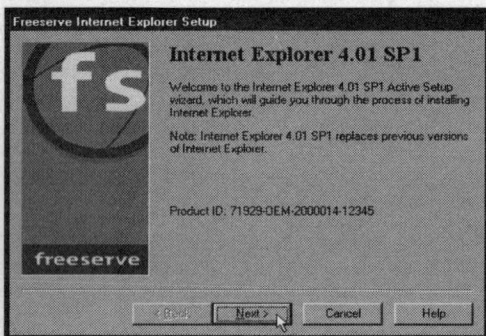

Freeserve – following the wizard

The Internet Explorer Active Setup 'wizard' now starts to guide you through the set-up process. Because you can only have one version of Internet Explorer installed, it will replace your existing version, so there is no reason to worry if you already have IE4 installed on your PC (it is automatically installed with Windows 98). Click 'Next' to continue.

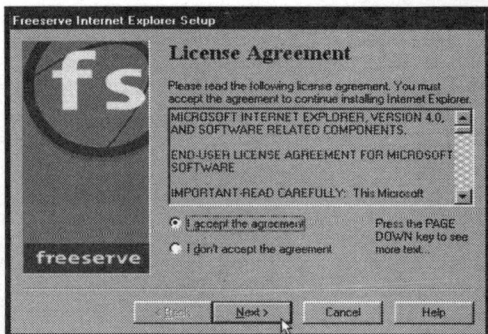

Freeserve – agreeing to the license

The next step is the license agreement, which explains the conditions under which you can use the Freeserve copy of Internet Explorer 4. Most people ignore the agreement and simply click on the 'I accept the agreement' option. Then click on the 'Next' button, which takes you to the next stage of the installation procedure.

20

Freeserve Internet Explorer Setup

Installation Option

Select the installation option you prefer, and then click Next.

Freeserve Minimal Installation

Freeserve Minimal Installation
Freeserve Standard Installation
Freeserve Full Installation
  Web browser and Outlook Express.

Internet Explorer 4.01 SP1 Setup automatically verifies and
downloads software created by Microsoft.

freeserve

< Back   Next >   Cancel   Help

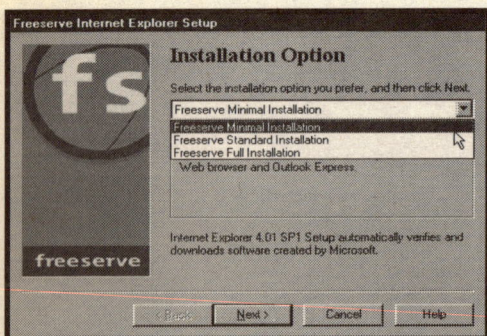

Freeserve – choosing the version

You are now asked to choose between three options
for installing the Freeserve copy of Internet Explorer.
If you have the older version of Internet Explorer on
your PC, version 3, then you should go for the full
installation. If you have Internet Explorer 4, as most
readers will have, select 'Standard' or 'Minimum.'

21

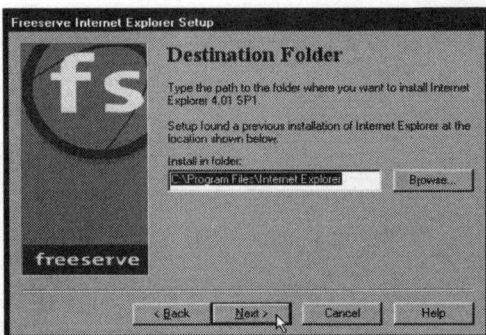

Freeserve – choosing the destination

Now you are asked to select the destination folder for IE4 (note that all existing versions of the programs will be replaced). You can specify where exactly on your hard drive you want the whole of IE4 to go, but our advice would be to leave the file path as it is and click on the 'Next' button.

22

Freeserve Internet Explorer Setup

Setup has finished installing components.

If you are connected to the Internet, please disconnect now. Setup must close all programs to finish the installation.

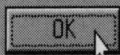

[OK]

Freeserve – starting the installation

The installation wizard now goes in to automatic mode and starts the installation process. You will have to wait until the next prompt appears. After a few minutes – or longer, depending on which installation you picked – a message appears telling you the installation is complete. Click on the 'OK' button.

23

```
Internet Explorer 4.01 SP1 Setup

    [globe]    Configuring system. Please wait...


           Preparing to run Internet Explorer 4.01 SP1...
```

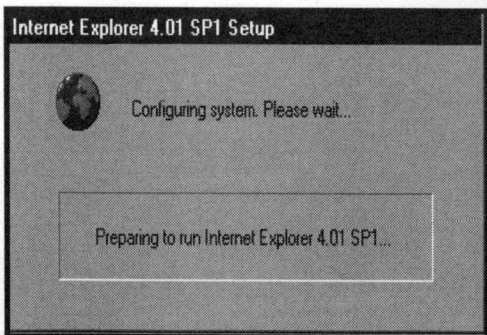

Freeserve – restarting the PC

The wizard again goes into automatic mode while it configures your system ready to run the new version of Internet Explorer. Wait for a while for a message telling you that the installer has to restart you computer. Click on the 'OK' button. After rebooting, the set-up program will run automatically in Windows 95. If you use Windows 98 or Windows NT, you will have to run the setup.exe program on the CD to continue

24

Freeserve – checking for right software

It is at this point that the Freeserve software checks your PC to see if it has the correct connection software installed on it already. Click on the 'Continue' button to proceed – that's all you should have to do.

25

free serve

Internet Setup

You are now ready to continue with the sign-up process.

Continue   Cancel

Freeserve – checking your modem's on

The software is now ready to sign you up with an account. Make sure your modem is switched on and plugged into your PC and click on the 'Continue' button to sign up with Freeserve and get on the Internet.

26

Internet Connection Wizard

Connecting

The Internet Connection Wizard will now connect to your Internet service provider.

Phone Number: 0 845 0796599

Dialing...

Cancel

Freeserve – dialling in

Now your modem should connect to the Freeserve registration server. If you have an x2, K56Flex or V.90 modem, the wizard may take a while to find the server this is a recognised bug at Freeserve's end, so don't worry, you are not doing anything wrong.

27

Welcome to

free serve

© Create a new account   <u>Click Here</u>

® Retrieve my account   <u>Click Here</u>

Help   Cancel

Freeserve – creating new account

A security alert pops-up, but don't be alarmed. It's just telling you that you have made a secure connection and nobody can intercept information you may send. Click on 'OK.' When the Freeserve logo appears you have a choice of creating a new account or retrieving an existing account. Click on the 'Create new account' link

28

free serve Acceptable Use Policy

Please read the following information carefully as it affects your rights and liability in law.

FREESERVE LIMITED

ACCEPTABLE USE POLICY

TERMS AND CONDITIONS

NOTICE: You must read these terms and conditions before
accessing Freeserve. By accessing Freeserve you agree to

Back   Help   Cancel   Accept

Accept

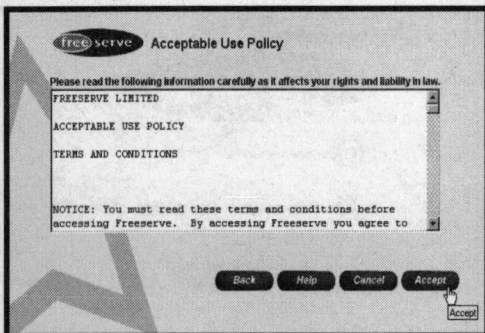

Freeserve – more terms and conditions

Another terms and conditions message appears. It's actually worth reading this one because it outlines some quite serious legal warnings. Read the information and click on 'Accept' if you are willing to abide by the policy.

29

free serve	Personal Information

First Name ___Clive___ Surname ___Hollister___ Male ⦿ Female ⦿

Date of birth Day 9 ▾ Month July ▾ Year 1966 Marital status Single ▾

Address _____

TownCity _____

Post Code _____

Household interests ☐ Arts and Culture ☐ Computer Games ☐ Cars
Click all that apply ☐ Horoscopes ☐ Business & Investment ☑ Technology
☐ Sports ☑ Pets ☐ Outdoor Pursuits
☑ Music ☐ Exhibitions & Museums ☑ Books
☑ Shopping ☑ Travelling ☐ Cooking
☐ Gambling ☐ News & Current Events ☑ Cinema

Income Select ▾ Current internet connection Select ▾

How did you hear about Freeserve? Select ▾ Where did you obtain the Freeserve CD? Select ▾

Occupation Select ▾ Highest level of education Select ▾

This information may be passed to other organisations who may, from time to time, contact you about products and services you may be interested in. If you do not wish to take advantage of this service, please click in this box. ☐

(Back) (Help) (Cancel) (Continue)

Freeserve – providing personal details

Now you have to enter your personal details so the account can be set up. This form usually takes a couple of minutes to fill in. Make sure you use all the fields, then click on 'Continue.' Make sure you click the tiny box at the bottom which stop you from receiving promotional material from Dixons and its partners (unless you want it, of course).

30

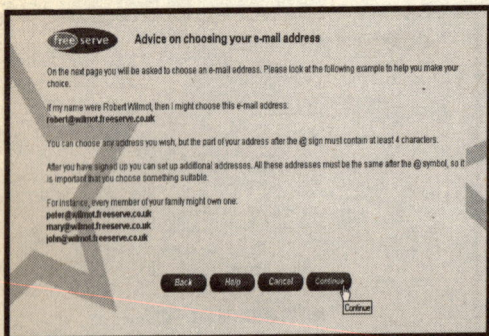

Freeserve – setting up your email address

The next screen explains how your Freeserve email address will be constructed. It's a good idea to put your first name before the @ symbol and your last name after, so your email address would read firstname@lastname.freeserve.co.uk. Just make sure you pick something that's easy to remember.

Freeserve – choosing email password

The next screen is where you enter your email details and choose a password. Make sure that you choose a password that you will be able to remember, or you will be locked out of your account. When you have done this, click on 'Continue.'

32

Internet Connection Wizard

Please record the following information for future use.

Account Name: .freeserve.co.uk
Password:

OK

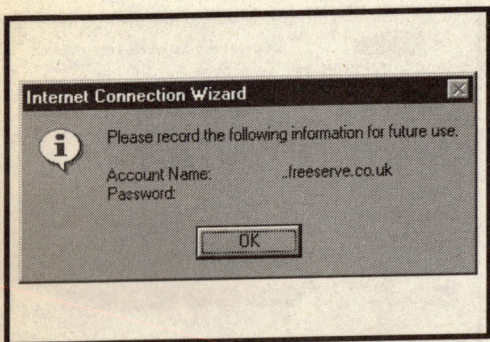

Freeserve – confirming your password

The next screen displays your email address and Freeserve user name. We've blanked the details out in this image, for security reasons. Click on 'Continue.' An alert message pops up to remind you of your Freeserve account name and password. Make a note of these details so you can get back online. Click on the 'OK' button to continue.

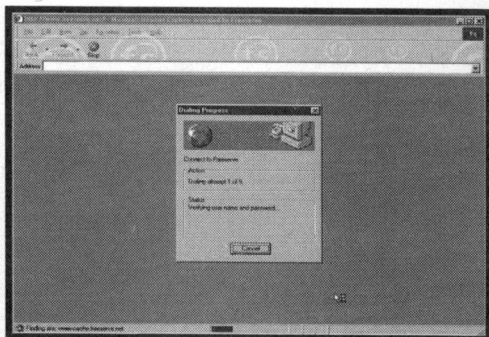

Freeserve – connecting to the Internet

The final alert appears telling you are ready to connect to the Internet. Click on the 'OK' button, then double-click on the Internet icon (or the Internet Explorer icon) on your desktop to connect to the Internet. When you launch Internet Explorer 4, it automatically dials the Freeserve number and passes your username and password to the Freeserve server. You don't have to do anything else to log on. The Freeserve Web site should then appear, indicating that you made a Net connection.

34

```
Dial-Up Networking
File   Edit   View   Connections   Help
  Make New Connection
  Freeserve
  FreeZone Internet
  Global Internet
  NetDirect
```

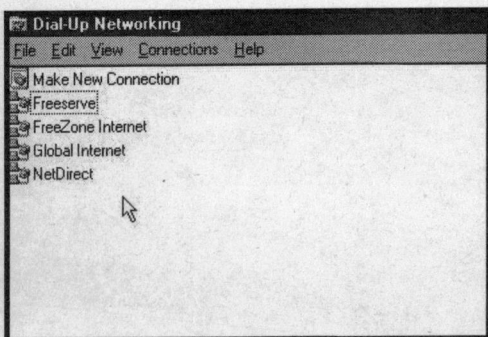

Setting up ISP accounts manually

While most ISPs get you to install their Web-browser based software to set up the account, you can also set up most accounts using Windows Dial-Up Networking, saving you from having to install Internet Explorer 4 or updating your existing version. Dial-Up Networking is powerful software built into Windows that lets you connect to the Net via an ISP. All you'll usually need from your service provider is a username, password and dial-up number for a modem.

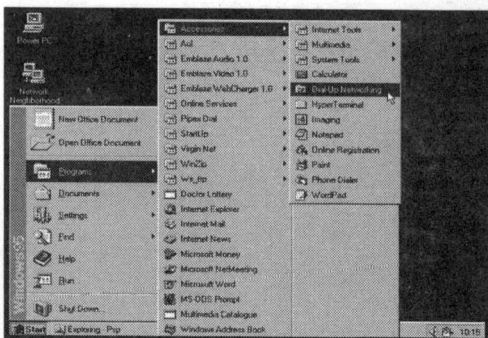

Finding Dial-Up Networking

You find Dial-Up Networking going to the Start button on the Windows 95 or Windows 98 Taskbar. Once there, select Programs, then Accessories, then open Dial-Up Networking. Alternatively, double-click 'My Computer' and the Dial-Up Networking folder should appear. If not, see tip 41.

36

Make New Connection

Type a name for the computer you are dialing:

Global Internet

Select a modem:

Sportster Flash 33.6 (UK) External

Configure...

< Back   Next >   Cancel

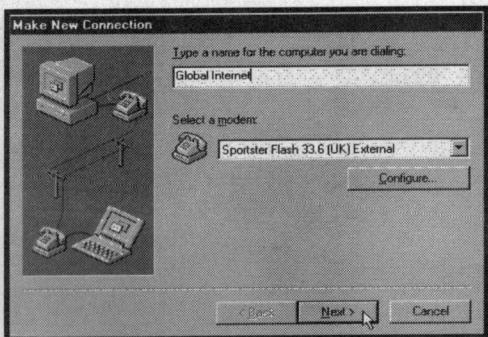

Making new connection

To make a new connection to your ISP, open the
Dial-Up Networking folder and click on the Make
New Connection icon. In the Make New Connection
box, enter the name of the service provider you
want to connect to and make sure that your modem
is selected from the drop down list.

Make New Connection

Type the phone number for the computer you want to call:

Area code:
0845

Telephone number:
079 8787

Country code:
United Kingdom (44)

< Back   Next >   Cancel

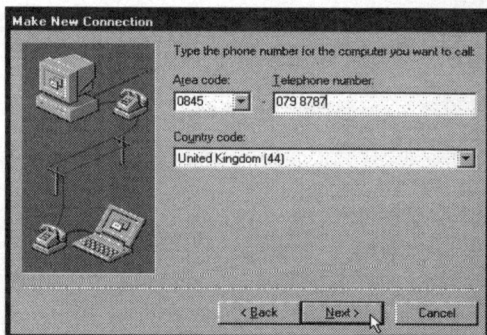

Entering the right number

Now enter the dial-up phone number of the service provider. If you've got a 56kbps modem, make sure you've got the right dial-up number to connect at this speed – phone up the technical support desk or see the company's Web site. Some service providers still have separate numbers for 56kbps modem and slower ones, so you need the right one to get a fast Internet connection. Also check with your ISP that it supports V.90 modems if you have one. If not, we would recommend switching to an ISP that does support this fast modem technology – AOL, Virgin Net or Freeserve, for example.

38

Dial-Up Networking

Make New Connection | Virgin Net | Pipex Dial | Global Internet

4 object(s)

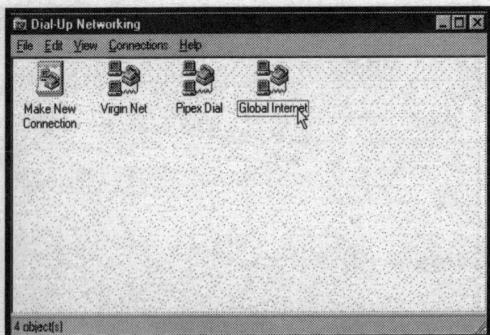

Finishing the installation

The final screen lets you edit the service provider name once more. If everything is OK, click the Finish button. The new dial-up connection appears in the Dial-Up Networking window. Now double-click on your new connection to log on.

39

```
┌─ Connect To ──────────────────── ? ☒
│  ┌─┐
│  ┃   Global Internet
│  └─┘
│
│  User name:    cparker
│  Password:     xxxxxx
│                ☑ Save password
│
│  Phone number: 0 845 0798787
│  Dialing from: Default Location ▼   Dial Properties...
│                        ┌─────────┐
│                        │ Connect │   Cancel
│                        └─────────┘
└────────────────────────────────────────
```

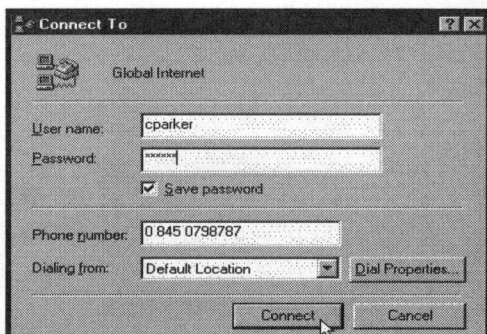

Entering your details

Enter your user name or user ID as supplied by the
service provider in the User name box, then enter
your password in the Password box. If you want to
save the password so you don't have to enter it
again, click on the Save password box. Now click on
the Connect button to connect to the Internet. Use
this method to set up as many Internet accounts as
you wish

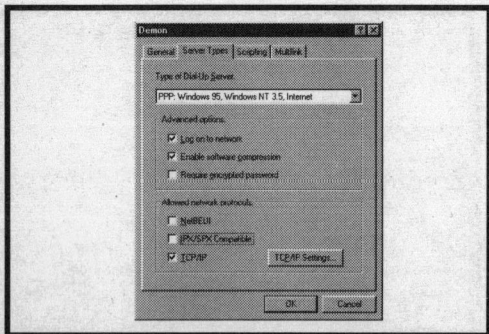

Connecting quicker with Dial-Up Networking

You can reduce the amount of time it takes Dial-Up
Networking to make a connection by right-clicking
your ISP icon in the DUN folder and choosing
Properties from the menu. In Server Types, untick
NetBEUI and IPX/SPX. These are advanced network
settings that home Net users don't need.

41

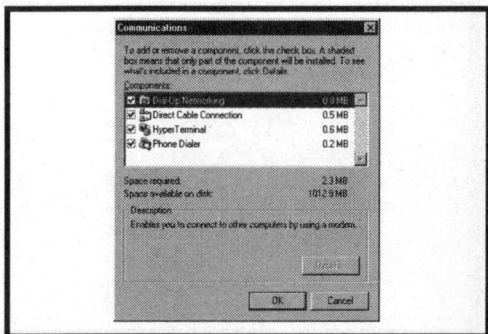

Wot, no Dial-Up Networking?

If Dial-Up Networking doesn't appear under the 'My Computer' folder or via the Start menu, run the 'Add/Remove Software' Control Panel, select 'Windows Setup,' then 'Communication,' then 'Details' and check the 'Dial-Up Networking' box. Click on 'OK.' Windows will then install it and you can set up accounts from ISPs in the way just described.

42

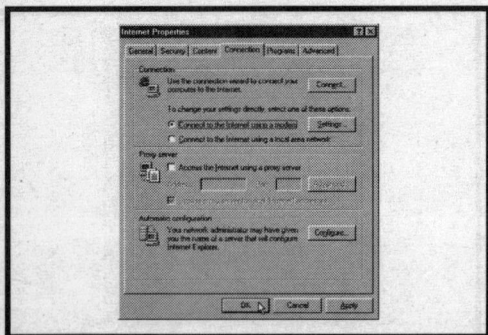

Log-on instantly

You should be able to connect to the Net automatically when you run your Web browser or check for email messages. If not, go to the Start button in the Taskbar and select Control Panel. Now open the 'Internet' Control Panel and click on the 'Connection' tab. In the connection box at the top of the window, make sure that the button marked 'Connect to the Internet using a modem' is selected.

```
Connect To                                    ? X

        Pipex X2

User name:    UK/soldd32
Password:     ********
              ☑ Save password

Phone number: 0 845 0885576
Dialing from: Portishead        ▼   Dial Properties...

                        Connect        Cancel
```

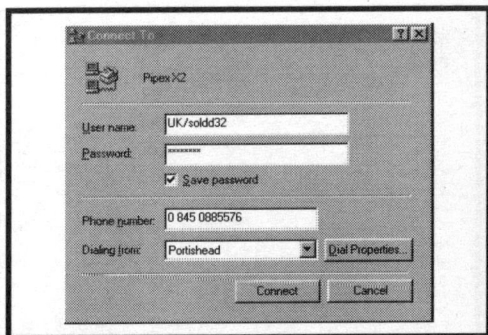

Forget the password

If you don't want to type in your password every
time you log onto the Internet, use the Save
password option in the Connect To window of the
Dial-Up Networking dialler. Go to My Computer and
double-click on it, then double-click on the Dial-Up
Networking icon and then double-click on the
connection you want to modify. Type your password
into the Password field then click on the Save
password box. Repeat for any other accounts you
may have.

44

What modem to buy

It isn't worth saving money by buying a slow, non-Hayes compatible or poorly featured modem. Go for the best you can get, a 56kbps V.90 device with fax and voice (answerphone) features. Make sure it's 'flash ROM upgradeable' so you can easily upgrade it to any future modem standards, without having to set it back to the manufacturer. Either external or internal modems are OK, though external modems are easier for beginners to set up.

45

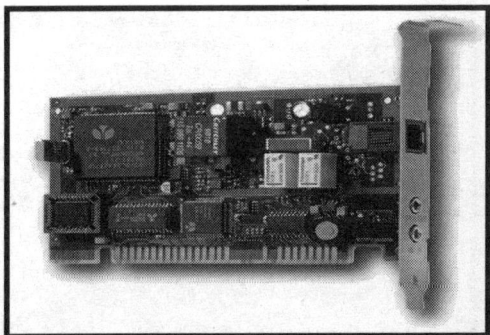

Internal modems – pros and cons

Internal modems are cheaper and tidier, and leave your second serial port free, though you'll probably have to set the modem to work on COM3 and put your mouse on COM2 (assuming you don't have a separate mouse port). Windows can get a bit upset if you have a COM1, COM2 and COM4 with no COM3 – whatever the documentation says. Most new PCs come with internal modems. You plug one end of the phone line into the back of the PC, the other into the phone socket.

46

Add New Hardware Wizard

Select the type of hardware you want to install.

Hardware types:

- CD-ROM controllers
- Display adapters
- Floppy disk controllers
- Global positioning devices
- Hard disk controllers
- Infrared
- Keyboard
- Memory Technology Drivers (MTDs)
- Modem
- Mouse

< Back   Next >   Cancel

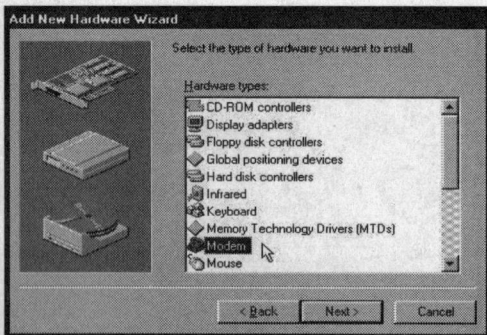

Checking your modem

Windows should find your new modem
automatically if you run 'Add New Hardware' from
'Control Panel.' When it does, you can check its
settings in the Modem Control Panel to make sure it
got it right. If Windows doesn't find it, or gets it
wrong, check the modem is turned on and
connected to the PC (if external), to the phone
socket, is set up correctly (if internal) and doesn't
conflict with anything else on your system – most
often a COM port.

47

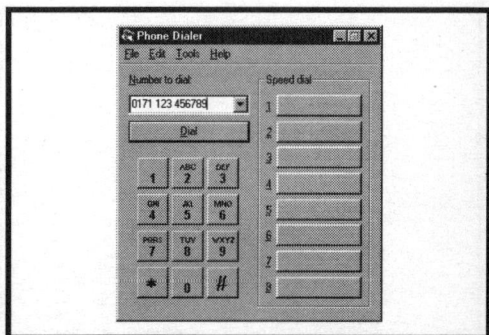

Modem recognition problems

If Windows fails to find your external modem, try telling it you have a 'Standard modem,' which should work for any current PC modem. Check its operation using 'Dialer' (from 'Start' select 'Run' and type 'Dialer'). Type in any phone number and Dialer should use your modem to call it. If it rings it's working correctly.

48

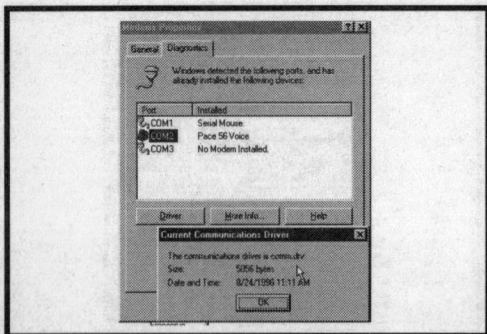

Get the right driver

One problem with setting the modem up as a
generic, standard device is that Windows won't
report its true connection speed. Once you have got
your modem set up as a standard device, you should
install the correct software 'driver' for your device
from the disk supplied, or download it from the
maker's Web site. Then install the driver in
Windows, using 'Add New Hardware' Control Panel.

```
comm 2 - HyperTerminal                                    _ □ ×
File Edit View Call Transfer Help
┌─────┬─────┬──────┬──────┬─────┬────┐
│     │     │      │      │     │    │

ati4
USRobotics Courier V.Everything Settings...

   B0   C1   E1   F1   M1   Q0   V1   X7
   SPEED=57600   TY=N   WORDLEN=8
   DIAL=PULSE   OFF LINE   TIMER

   &A3  &B1  &C1  &D2  &H1  &I0   &  &L0   &M4  &N0
   &R2  &S0  &T5  &U0  &X0  &Y1   %N6

   S00=000   S0   S02=043   S03=013   S04=010   S05=008   S0
   S08=004   S09=006   S10=014   S11=070   S12=050   S13=00
   S16=000   S17=000   S18=000   S19=00=000   S21=010   S22
   S24=150   S25=005   S26=001   S27=00=008   S29=020   S30
   S32=009   S33=000   S34=000   S35=000   S36=000   S370
   S40=000   S41=000   S42=126   S43=200   S44=015   S4000
   S48=000   S49=000   S50=000   S51=000   S52=000   S53=00

Connected 00:07:45   Auto detect   57600 8-N-1   SCROLL  CAPS  NUM  Capture
```

Configure skating

You might want to run diagnostic checks on your
modem, check settings or simply set the volume – so
you need to be able to send commands to the
modem rather than use it to connect to the Net. The
manual supplied with your modem lists the
commands it understands.

Start 'HyperTerminal' ('Accessories' on the 'Start'
menu) and create a new connection called 'Fake' (or
whatever). The 'Phone Number' dialogue screen
appears. Click the 'down' arrow on the 'Connect
Using' box and select the COM port your modem is
on. That's it. Now you can type commands straight
into your modem. If you type 'ATZ' for example, it
should return 'OK.'.

50

Pace 56 Voice Properties ? ×

General | Connection | **Options** | Distinctive Ring | Forwarding

Connection control
- ☐ Bring up terminal window before dialing
- ☑ Bring up terminal window after dialing

Dial control
- ☐ Operator assisted or manual dial

Wait for credit card tone: 8 ⬍ seconds

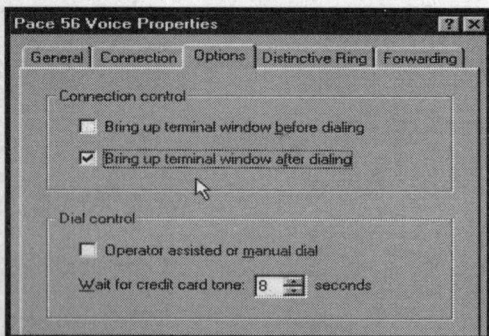

Can't connect, won't connect

It's irritating when your modem dials the right
number, finds the ISP's modem and then drops the
line again. Open Dial-Up Networking and select the
icon for the ISP connection you're using. On the
'File' menu click 'Properties,' then 'Configure' and
then the 'Options' tab. Tick the 'Bring Up Terminal
Window After Dialing' box. You should now be able
to see what's happening. Are you using the right ID?
(some ISPs require a slightly different ID if using
software other than their own.) Is the password
correct and in the right case? Are you selecting the
right protocol – PPP, normally?

5 1

```
TCP/IP Settings                          ? X

  ○ Server assigned IP address
  ○ Specify an IP address

     IP address:        0 . 0 . 0 . 0

  ○ Server assigned name server addresses
  ○ Specify name server addresses

     Primary DNS:       0 . 0 . 0 . 0
     Secondary DNS:     0 . 0 . 0 . 0
     Primary WINS:      0 . 0 . 0 . 0
     Secondary WINS:    0 . 0 . 0 . 0
```

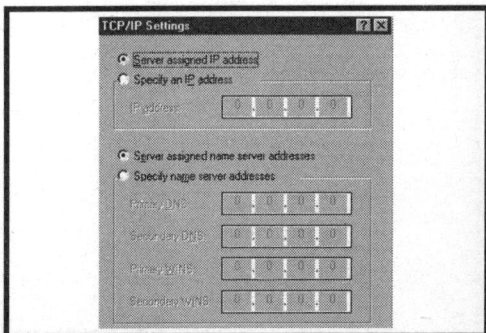

More in-depth tests

If these items are correct, check the TCP/IP settings
(From Dial-Up Networking right click the connection,
select 'Properties' and 'Server Type,' then 'TCP/IP
Settings.') You can also check the Networks Control
Panel for more obscure TCP/IP settings if your service
provider needs them. If all else fails, get the ISP's
help desk to guide you through a new Dial-Up
Networking set-up.

52

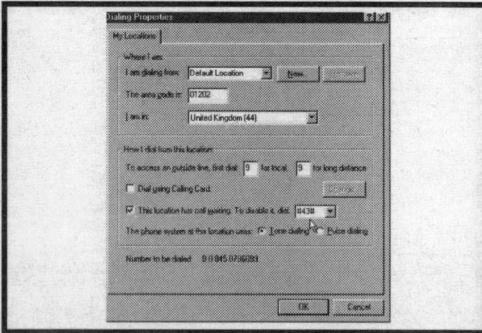

Curing dropped lines

One of the major problems experienced by new dial-up Net users is mysteriously dropped connections. The most common reason for this is BT's Call Waiting service. It interrupts your call for half a second to beep at your modem, which then assumes that the connection is permanently lost. You have two options: cancel Call Waiting with BT (ring 150 for customer service) or have Dial-Up Networking disable it when you call. To do this, double-click on the connection in Dial-Up Networking and select 'Dial Properties.' Click in 'This Location Has Call Waiting' and type in the sequence '#43#'. This disables it.

53

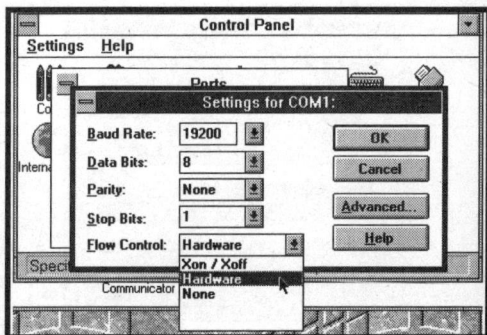

Speeding up modems in Windows 3.x

Still using Windows 3.x? Chah! For high-speed modem connections under Windows 3.x, set the serial port to use hardware handshaking (CTS/RTS) by going into Control Panels and choose the Ports. Double-click on the port your modem is connected to then click on the Settings button. Finally, select the pop-up Hardware option under Flow Control. Selecting Hardware flow control in Windows 3.x can increase your connection speed to the Internet

54

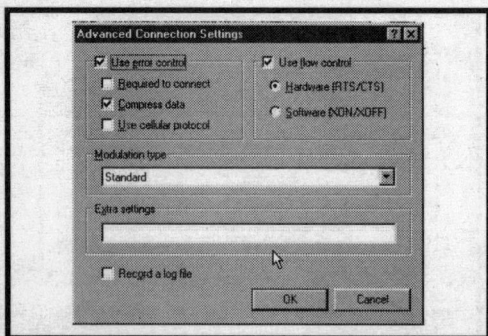

Add commands

If you need to pass 'AT' commands to your modem
in addition to those Windows already sends, open
the Modems Control Panel, select your modem, click
the Properties button, select the Connection tab,
click on Advanced then enter the string in the 'Extra
Settings' box. Be sure to use AT at the beginning of
the command string because Windows won't add
this command prefix for you.

55

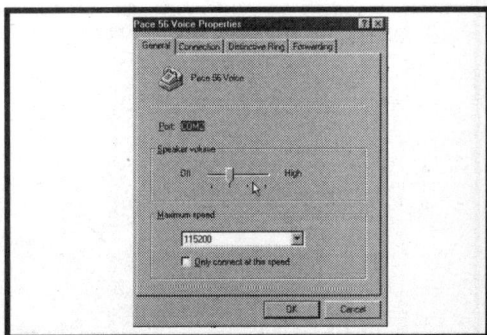

Be a good listener

Sometimes listening to your modem's attempt to
connect to a service provider can help you track a
problem. You may be connecting to a voice line
instead of a modem, for instance, in which case
you'll hear a person answer. You can turn on your
modem's speaker by setting the options or sending
the ATL3 command when initialising the modem
from most communications programs. Use the
method in the previous tip to add the command to
the Connection setup.

56

Pace 56 Voice Properties

General | Connection | Distinctive Ring | Forwarding

Pace 56 Voice

Port: COM3

Speaker volume

Off ——|—— High

Maximum speed

115200

☐ Only connect at this speed

OK   Cancel

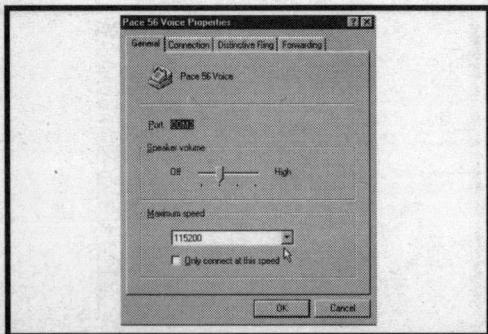

Go as fast as you can

Your 28.8/33.6/56kbps modem should be able to
handle a 115,200bps connection from your
computer, but Windows 95 typically communicates
with these modems at 57,600bps. To correct this,
open the Modem Control Panel, click on Properties
and select 115,200bps as the maximum speed. If this
causes problems, set the maximum speed back to
57,600bps.

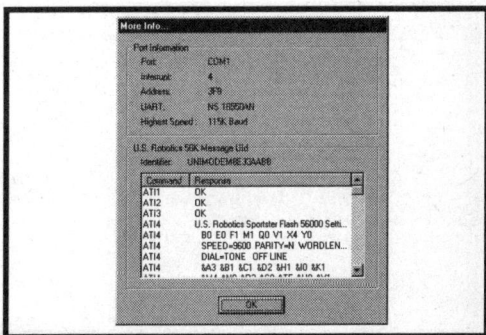

Do Diagnostics

If you're not sure whether your modem is
responding to commands, open the Modem Control
Panel and select Diagnostics. Select your modem (if
it's internal) or the COM port (if it's external), and
click on the More Info. After a pause, you should see
a list of responses from the modem in the window.
If there is no list or an error message, check your
physical connections, and then the port and IRQ
settings for the modem (see the handbook) It's easy
to check for modem problems

58

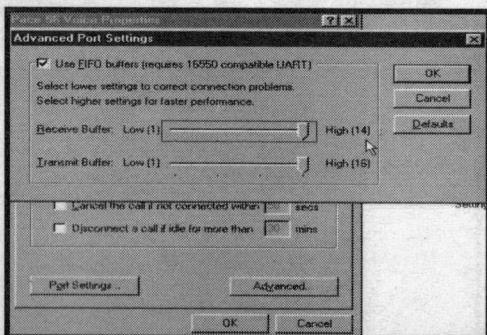

Work those chips

If you're working in Windows 95 and you have a
16550 UART chip governing your serial ports – most
Pentium-class PCs do – make sure you're getting
your modem's worth. Click Control Panel and select
Modems/Properties, then look under the Connection
tab for Port Settings. Check the 'Use FIFObuffers'
option and drag both sliders all the way to the right.
If that causes problems later, drag the sliders back a
little and initiate a new session. Repeat this
procedure until everything stabilises.

59

```
Connected to Freeserve                    ? X

      Connected at 31,200 bps              [  OK  ]
      Duration: 000:00:23
      Bytes received: 847                  [ Disconnect ]
      Bytes sent: 2,024
                                           [ Details >> ]


 Paint Sh..   Dial-Up ...   Conne...              15:34
```

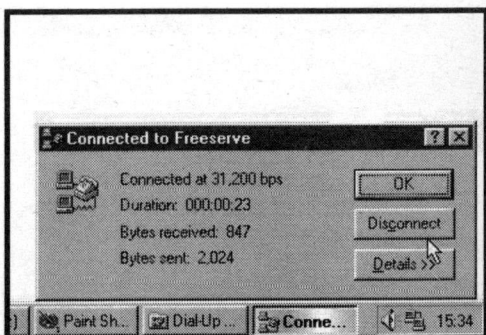

Reset the software

When modem problems arise, a quick fix is to switch
the modem off and on to reset it. This is perfectly
OK, but you should also reinitialise the modem using
your communications software. If you don't, the
modem will institute its default profile of
commands, but that may not include commands
needed by your software. So switch off the modem
and exit from your Internet software or dialler, then
switch on the modem and run the software again.

60

Connected to Freeserve

Connected at 31,200 bps		OK
Duration: 000:01:10		Disconnect
Bytes received: 847		No Details
Bytes sent: 2,024		

Modem: Pace 56 Voice
Server type: PPP: Windows 95, Windows NT 3.5, Internet
Protocols:

1) TCP/IP

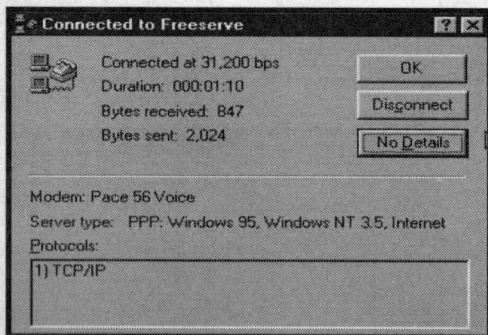

Remember compression

It can be confusing when Dial-Up Networking or
other dialler software reports a connection speed
lower than the modem's rated maximum. This is
because the software usually displays the speed of
the telephone connection without taking software
and hardware 'compression' into account. So your
modem is usually downloading data at a higher rate
than is being displayed. But on the other hand, your
Web browser could show you downloading data at
rates higher than specified by your modem, so you
can actually download data at 70kbps or 80kbps a
second using a 56kbps modem.

CHAPTER TWO

EMAIL

Email is the 'killer application' for the Internet, providing a fast and efficient method of communication all around the world. Email software is pretty easy to use, too. Like most software, you can't do any damage by playing with an email program, so it's a good idea to experiment by sending test messages – to us, for example. Here are some tips to get you started...

61

S	P	A	Label	Who	Date	K	V	Subject
F				cc18 - Course U	13:56 22/11/96	1		Eyelid Producti
	•			PIPEX Dial Supp	21:26 24/11/96	3		Re: where's my
				Postmaster@int	17:56 02/12/96	3		Undeliverable M
				Life.Is.Short@m	18:17 02/01/97	7		Huh?
⬆		☐		Subnet Ltd	17:23 07/01/97	2		Club 18-30 holic
▲				Subnet Ltd	13:49 08/01/97	5		Subnet Ltd pres
				Subnet Ltd	13:51 08/01/97	4		Cyberotic Zone
				Mail Delivery Sul	19:49 15/01/97	3		Returned mail:
				Phil Parker	17:16 31/01/97	6		Number Nine Te
				Electronic Postn	14:08 08/02/97	54		Undeliverable m
42/677K/1K								

Hanging on to email

Unlike paper mail (snail mail), email is copied rather
than sent, so it can exist in several places. The sender
has the original; your ISP has the first copy. When
you download email from your ISP, another copy
comes to you. At this point your email software can
tell the ISP's mail server (a big networked computer
which processes email) to delete its copy – the
normal default setting. This leaves just the sender's
copy and yours in existence (as well as freeing up
disk space on your ISP's mail servers).Email software
normally keeps all messages in a database file until
you delete them – you can keep emails for years!

62

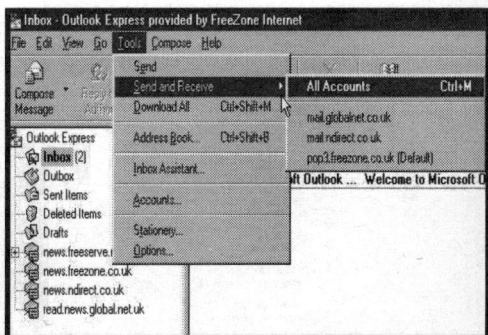

Delivery times

Email is handled on the Internet in what's called a
'store and forward' fashion. It has a relatively low
priority. Usually it's delivered in a minute or two,
irrespective of where it's going in the world, though
on really bad days it can take hours. If the mail
server at the other end is having problems it won't
be delivered until the other end is fixed – though
you'll usually get a message from your ISP's mail
server telling you it will try at regular intervals for a
certain number of days if mail can't be delivered
immediately. At the other end, the recipient usually
has to collect their email – another variable you
can't control. If information must be imparted right
now, make a phone call.

63

| find people | web search | join bigfoot | email tools | tour bigfoot | member's area |

Geoff Harris (Go)   new search | modify search | search the web

E-mail Results 1 - 23 of 23

1) HARRIS, GEOFF
gharris908@aol.com

2) HARRIS, GEOFF
gwh@therker.com

3) Harris, Geoff
G.Harris@boro.ac.uk

4) Harris, Geoff
harriso@ok.com

5) HARRIS, GEOFF
gwh@flash.net

6) HARRIS, GEOFF
harris@meena.co.uregina.ca

7) HARRIS, GEOFF
geoffh@paragon.co.uk

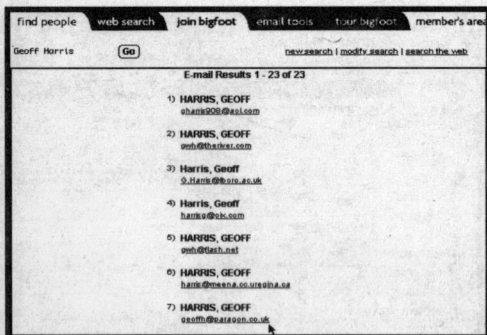

How to find an email address

Sad to say in this information age, the easiest way to find someone's email address is to ring up and ask them. There's no central list of email addresses on the Net, and anyway, addresses usually alter when people change their ISP or job. There are a number of email address registers that you and others can join. One of the biggest is Bigfoot (http://www.bigfoot.com). Try also WhoWhere, at http://www.whowhere.com/.

More email searching advice

You can also use the same search sites you use for finding Web sites – Excite (http://www.excite.com) and Yahoo! (Http://www.yahoo.co.uk) have good email location features. Another option is to see if the person sends messages to newsgroups. Go to the DejaNews Web site at http://www.dejanews.com and do a search on their name. If they do contribute to newsgroups, you should see their email address, though there's no guarantee it's the most current one.

65

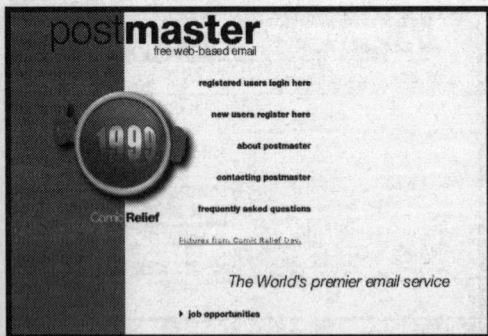

postmaster
free web-based email

registered users login here

new users register here

about postmaster

contacting postmaster

frequently asked questions

Pictures from Comic Relief Day.

Comic Relief

The World's premier email service

▸ job opportunities

How do I pick up email from anywhere?

Easy. First, you can sign up for a Web-based email account from a provider like HotMail (http://www.hotmail.com) or Postmaster (http://www.postmaster.co.uk) You can then send and receive your mail with any computer connected to the Net. Alternatively, you can set up your existing email account on any computer connected to the Net, so long as your service provider has a POP3 server (most have). All you need is an email program, the names of your ISP's mail servers, your ISP username and your password.

66

[S] PIPEX Dial services

services

E-web enables our customers with Dial-up accounts to read and delete e-mail from their account via any Web browser. This often proves useful whilst away from the office at someone else's computer.

Enter your **account name** (without the three letter prefix, e.g. smt99) or multiple mailbox name (not an alias) and your **password** in the boxes below and then click on the Login button. (Please note that you must **click on the Login button**, rather than simply pressing enter or return).

Log In

mail
name

password

Log in to Mail Service

Options

Read 1st 100 messages

○ read latest first
○ read earliest first

○ delete confirmation
○ no delete confirmation

Filter

keyword

○ Filter out
○ Filter in

○ Subject
○ From

ISP email on the Web

Don't forget that some bigger ISPs, PIPEX Dial for example, maintain an email Web page. Go to the page using a Web browser from any computer, type in your ID and password and you can read your email. If you think you'll need this sort of service check before subscribing. Or sign up for a free Web email account.

67

UNISYN | Order | Download | Support | Press | Company

SpamEx

Free Trial Download

Purchase SpamEx™

Report a Spammer

The #1 SPAM Filtration Tool
(now with multi-account support)

With just a click of a button you can deal with all your junk
mail. Or just have SpamEx™ scan automatically!

With Unisyn Spam Exterminator you will never have to deal
with these time-wasting messages again - plus, we give you
the power to fight back!

Free Trial Version

Everyone hates those unsolicited and annoying messages
that find their way into your e-mail. These messages can
range from advertisements for things you have no need for,
to blatant and illegal scam operations attempting to get at
your personal information or credit cards.

How do I avoid junk email, or spam?

You can't, not totally anyway. If you're at all active
on the Net you will eventually get some junk email –
ads and offers of various kinds. Just delete them.
Never respond except with a request to be taken off
the mailing list. If you are determined to stop it, try
one of the anti-spam programs on our CD, such as
Spam Exterminator.

68

```
▭▭▭▭▭▭▭▭▭▭▭▭▭▭▭▭▭▭▭▭▭▭▭▭  Alternate

General Augusto Pinochet
Former Dictator
Santiago
Chile

email: generalp@chile.com
Web site: www.pinochet.com

"Next time, I'll get my corns done at home!"
```

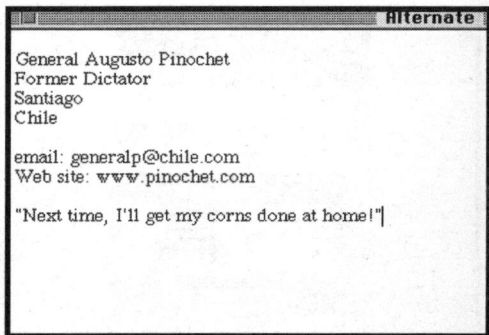

Automatically adding details to an email

If you get tired of typing out your details on every email, it makes sense to give all your mail a 'signature.' A signature is an extra bit of text tacked on to the end of every email you send, such as your phone and fax number along with your Web site, for example. Signatures are usually created in your email program and stored as text files. As a rule, keep them short and change those intended to be amusing frequently. See the Help section of your email program for details of adding signatures.

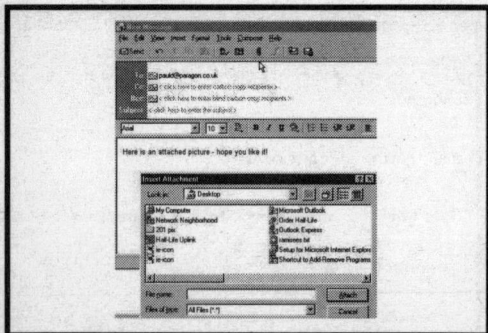

Attaching files to email

The easiest way to do this is to 'attach' a document
– simply click on the paper clip icon in your email
program, or click 'Attach' in the relevant menu.
Modern email programs use MIME (Multipurpose
Internet Mail Extensions) to handle email
attachments. In theory, any file attached to an email
using MIME can be handled by any other MIME
enabled program – and for Net users it usually
works fine. All modern email programs, such as
Eudora or Outlook Express, support MIME. Upgrade
yours from our CD if you have an old one.

70

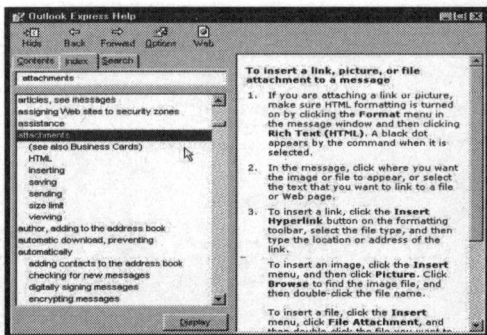

Easing attachment headaches

The system can break down if your message has to go through a mail gateway to or from a private network. These often use proprietary email systems. 'cc:mail' for example, is popular with major companies. Exchanging files with people on CompuServe and AOL can cause problems, as well, particularly if they're using old versions. There's no general fix when it doesn't work. Solutions often depend on the other end's network administrator or deep technical knowledge. If the problem is with a one-off attachment, it's simpler to send the file on disk. Using a modern email program should help.

71

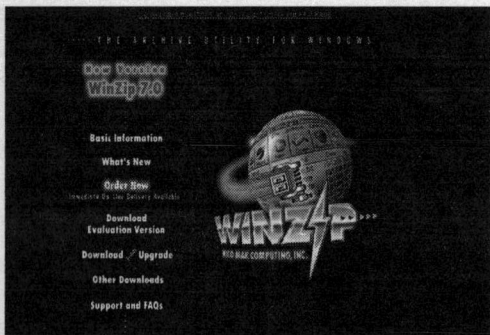

Compress big attachments

As we've seen, sending, or 'attaching,' a file from your PC along with an email message is one of the best ways to get documents or image files to people. It's worth shrinking, or 'compressing' big files using a program such as WinZip (PC) or StuffIt (Mac), so they're transmitted faster. Both programs are on our CD. If you save the compressed attachments as a self-extracting archive, anyone will be able to open the attachments without having to install WinZip or StuffIt as well.

72

```
Mime-Version: 1.0
Date: Thu, 17 Sep 1998 09:36:50 +0000
To: global@paragon.co.uk
From: damian butt <gecko@www2.paragon.co.uk>
Subject: Virus!
Status:

> Please Note
>
> Someone is sending out a very desirable screen-saver, the
> Budweiser Frogs - "BUDDYLST.ZIP". If you download it, you will lose
> everything!!! Your hard drive will crash and someone from the Internet
> will get your screen name and password! DO NOT DOWNLOAD THIS UNDER ANY
> CIRCUMSTANCES!!!! IT JUST WENT INTO circulation yesterday, as far as we
> know. Please distribute/inform this message.
> This is a new, very malicious virus and not many people know
> about it.
> This information was announced yesterday morning from Microsoft.
> Please share it with everyone that might access the Internet. Once
> again, pass this along to EVERYONE in your address book so that this
> may be stopped. Also do not open or even look at any mail that says
> "RETURNED OR UNABLE TO DELIVER". This virus will attach itself to
> your
> computer
> components and render them useless. Immediately delete mail items that
> say this. AOL has said that this is a very dangerous virus and that
> there is NO remedy for it at this time. Please practice cautionary
> measures and forward this to all you on-line friends ASAP.
>  <<Forward.txt>>
```

Dangerous attachment alert!

You shouldn't open attached files from Internet
users you don't know, as they may be infected by
viruses. Even if your email program does download a
dodgy-sounding attachment, don't worry too much.
It can only cause damage to your computer if you
'execute' or open the file. Be careful with Microsoft
Word documents, as well. The best policy for any
Internet user is to install some anti-virus software,
which will check attachments and other files
received from the Net. See the McAfee site at
http://www.mcafee.com/ or Dr Solomon's at
http://www.drsolomons.com/.

73

```
Mail Delivery Subsy. 12:08 10/02/97 +0, Returned mail: User unknown

Subject:  Returned mail: User unknown

Return-Path: <>
Date: Mon, 10 Feb 1997 12:08:32 +0100
From: Mail Delivery Subsystem <MAILER-DAEMON@betty.direct.it>
Subject: Returned mail: User unknown
To: <dsawyer@dial.pipex.com>

The original message was received at Mon, 10 Feb 1997 12:08:24 +0100
from maelstrom.dial.pipex.net [158.43.128.52]

    ----- The following addresses had delivery problems -----
ariete@mbox.vol.it  (unrecoverable error)
   (expanded from: <secure@systems.it>)

    ----- Transcript of session follows -----
... while talking to k100-fddi.mbox.vol.it.:
>>> RCPT To:<ariete@mbox.vol.it>
<<< 550 <ariete@mbox.vol.it>... User unknown
550 ariete@mbox.vol.it... User unknown

    ----- Original message follows -----
```

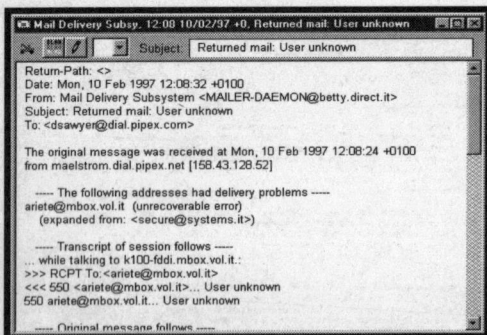

Why is my email being returned?

If it got no further than your own ISP then the address (the domain) doesn't exist (this is the part after the @ symbol). If it was returned from the mail server in the domain you sent it to, then the recipient doesn't exist. Alternatively, you may have spelt the recipient's name wrong, or put it in the wrong case. Or the email address may have changed since you last sent an email to the person (it happens).

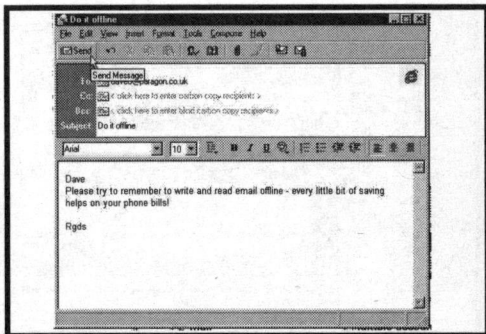

Write and read email offline

It's very tempting when you get your first batch of interesting email to reply to every message while you're still connected to the Net. The only trouble is, you're running up that phone bill by the minute. Try this. Run your email program without connecting to the Net, and compose the messages you want to send. When you've finished writing your messages, connect to the Internet and send and receive email. Now disconnect from the Internet and read your messages, composing any replies as you go. Once completed, connect to the Internet, send your mail then disconnect.

75

Messenger, the email part of Netscape Communicator, looks neat and works well

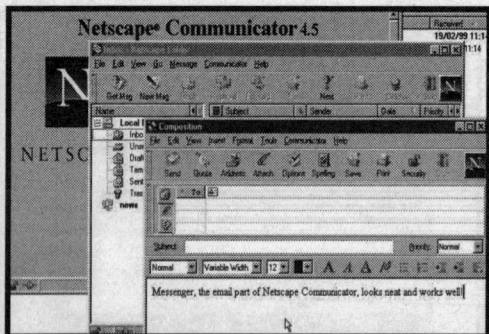

Use your Web browser

If you want to contact an email address on a Web
page, you don't have to write down the address and
then open a separate email program such as Eudora
to send the message. Using Internet Explorer or
Netscape Communicator, you can send an email
message by simply clicking on the email address on a
site. This opens a window in Outlook Express (using
Internet Explorer) or Netscape Messenger. Write
your message and click on the send button, and the
mail has been sent. Simple.

76

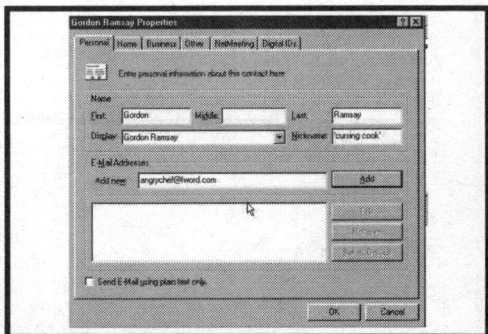

Organise an address book

Most email programs have a comprehensive address book for storing the addresses of the people you regularly contact. It's a good idea to keep the address book up to date, and with most programs you can do this automatically. In Outlook Express, double-click on a message to make it appear in a separate window. Now go to the Tools menu and select the Add To Address Book command and select Sender in the sub-menu. This puts the name and email address of the sender directly into the address book.

77

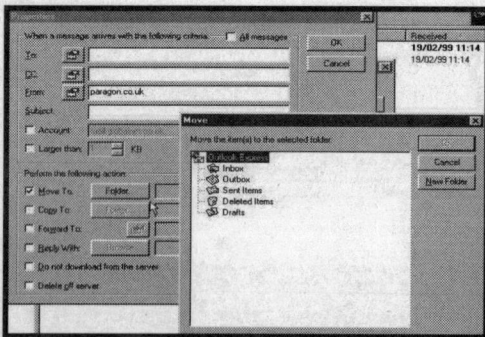

Filter your mail

If you have a family account with several different
email addresses, it's possible to filter mail so each
person's mail is stored in a separate folder. In
Outlook Express, create new mail folders for each
family member from the File menu of Outlook
Express. Now open the Inbox Assistant in the Tools
menu and click the Add button. In the Properties
box, type an email address in the To: field, then click
on the Move To: check box. Then, you click on the
Folder button. When the Move box appears, click on
the destination folder then click on the OK button.
Then, click OK in the Properties window.

78

Publicly Accessible Mailing Lists

Search results -- motorcycles

Get mailing lists for free

Don't get enough email? Try subscribing to a mailing list. Many Web sites on specific subjects let you subscribe to an Internet mailing list. This works in the same way as a conventional mailing list, except you're automatically sent email contributions to the list at regular intervals. You can search for mailing lists on your career, hobbies or preoccupations by going to the Liszt Web site at http://www.liszt.com/ or the List of Publicly Accessible Mailing Lists at http://www.neosoft.com/internet/paml/.

79

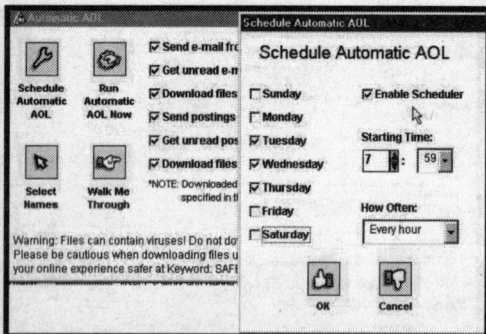

Work during offpeak hours

If you're using your email account from home, it's a good idea to send and receive your email during offpeak times (after 6pm, weekends) when charges are lower. This isn't quite as vital as it is with Web browsing because you're not online as long, but it's good Net practice nevertheless. AOL users should check out the comprehensive scheduling facilities for email, known as FlashSessions (Automatic AOL). In AOL 4.0i, click on the icon called 'Mail Room' and pick 'Set up Auto AOL.' Then follow the screens.

80

```
      To: reader@outsideworld.co.uk
    From: Geoff Harris <geoffh@paragon.co.uk>
 Subject: Email Netiquette
      Cc:
     Bcc:
X-Attachments:
...............................................................................
Dear Readers
Please don't type in upper case when you send an email –

IT'S THE EQUIVALENT OF SHOUTING!

Of course, if you want to SHOUT or add EMPHASIS, it's fine

Rgds
```

Use Netiquette

On the Internet, as in the real world, it pays to be polite. When sending email, use 'please' and 'thank you' in the same way as you would in a letter. Avoid sending libellous material in an email message – you can be sued just as effectively for an act of libel in an email as in a paper letter. Finally, don't type in capital letters except for effect – it's the email equivalent of SHOUTING – and don't send large image files attached to email messages unless it's absolutely necessary.

81

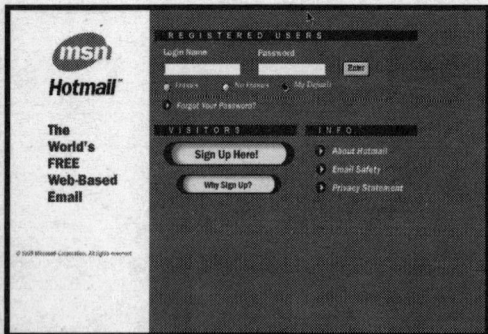

Get a free address

If you need more than one email address, or just
want a funkier one than jsmith@aol.com, you can
get a free email address off the Web. Try HotMail at
http://www.hotmail.com, Yahoo! mail at
http://www.yahoo.co.uk or Lycos mail at
http://www.lycos.co.uk Getting an email address this
way means that it will stay the same even if you
change service provider, and you can check your
email from any computer connected to the Net,
anywhere in the world.

82

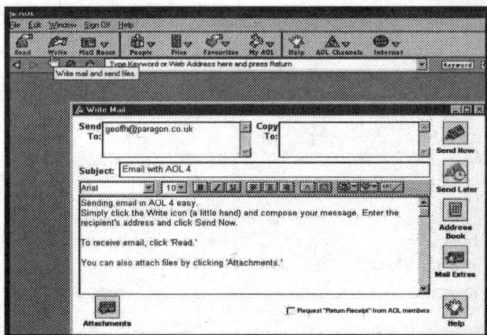

Email software and AOL

Since AOL doesn't use the POP3 email system used
by most Internet service providers (ISPs) you can't
use it with popular email programs such as Eudora
or Outlook Express. You're stuck with AOL's built-in
email system until the company supports POP3,
unfortunately. On the positive side, email is very
easy in AOL, especially in the new version, AOL 4.0i.

83

```
New Message
File  Edit  View  Insert  Format  Tools  Compose  Help
  Send Message Using          ▶    dial.pipex.com (Default)
  Send Later Using            ▶
  Save                             Lolicia's Freeserve email
  Save As...                       pop.freeserve.net
  Delete              Ctrl+D    rbon copy recipients >
  Move To Folder...            nd carbon copy recipients >
  Copy To Folder...            bject >
  Properties                        ▼   │ B  I  U  ⑨ │ ▐
  Close               Alt+F4
```

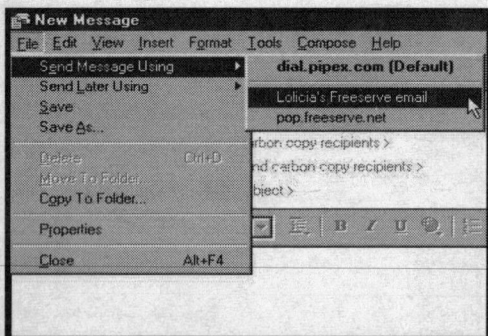

Cheap email only accounts

Even if you only want to use email and no other
Internet service, you should check out one of the
free ISPs, particularly Dixons' Freeserve. It offers
unlimited POP3 email addresses, which means that
you can set up an email account for every member
of the family. Just remember that it will cost 50p per
minute to call the help desk.

84

It's free, and offers something for everyone.

Netscape WebMail is supported by advertisers' banner ads, which are placed on top of every Netscape WebMail page.

All different types of people can benefit from the personal, private, and permanent email service.

Page Top Return to Sign Up

- **Mobile professionals** - Access your email from the road. You can even have Netscape WebMail collect your mail from other addresses.

- **Families with one email account or shared Internet access** - If you're tired of sharing your mailbox with others in your household, Netscape WebMail can give you a personal and private address.

- **Students** - Don't worry about losing your email address after you graduate. Netscape WebMail will supply you with a permanent address that will keep you in touch with your friends and family forever.

- **Teachers** - If you have more students than Internet access accounts, Netscape WebMail can give your students a free, fully functional email address in minutes!

- **Those without a computer** - Sign up with Netscape WebMail and you can have an email address on the Internet without buying a computer! You can access your email from a local library, an Internet café, or a friend's house, so you don't even need Internet access.

- **Those thinking of switching Internet service providers** - If you are thinking about switching your provider, you don't need to worry about losing your email address.

You need an all-in-one communications tool.

With Netscape WebMail Premium Services, you enjoy the most advanced email functionality on the Web. Premium Services offer you the convenience and freedom of Web-based email with the bells and whistles of a business email tool, all at competitive prices. Here's just a sampling of our Premium Services:

Page Top Return to Sign Up

- **POP Access** - Enjoy the advantages of Web-based email with the convenience of your favorite email client. With POP Access, you can POP or get your Netscape WebMail messages in your POP3-compliant email client (e.g. Netscape Messenger), offering you the ability to read and manage your mail offline.

- **Pager Notify** - Stay informed with Pager Notify. This service lets you know when new email arrives in your Netscape WebMail account, and even forwards some or all of a message to your pager's display.

- **Extra Storage** - You can purchase an additional 5 MB of memory for your Netscape WebMail account. This extra 5 MB allows you to store more mail and more attachments in your Netscape WebMail account!

Juggling accounts

Some Web-based email accounts will let you check
what email has been sent to an existing email
account you may have with an Internet service
provider (ISP). You may also be able to download
Web-based email to a POP3-based email program
(Outlook Express, for instance) so you can read it
offline.

85

Dear Auntie

I am writing this email offline in a word processor so I don't run up my phone bills writing it online. I can write as much as I want this way, lingering over every last linguistic nuance, and to hell with BT. Why I can even check the spelling and grammar.

Shame I can't think of anything else to write at the moment!

Your Loving Nephew

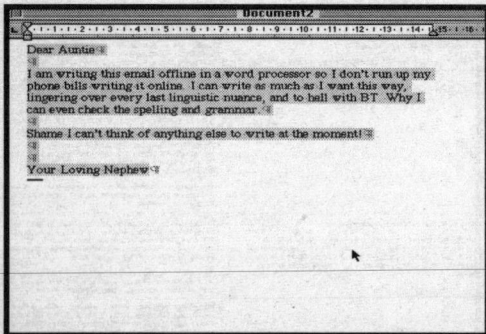

Working offline with Web-based email

Although standard Web-based email accounts don't let you do as much offline as you can with a POP3 account provided by your ISP, there is nothing to stop you writing the message offline in a word processor and then copying and pasting it into the Web email form and sending it. You can even paste email you have received into a word processor document in order to read the message offline.

86

```
X-Sender: dh46@pop.dial.pipex.com
Date: Thu, 04 Mar 1999 09:12:49 +0000
To: Geoff Harris <geoffh@paragon.co.uk>
From: steve patient <spatient@dial.pipex.com>
Subject: Re: Linux-owered MP3 player for cars
Mime-Version: 1.0
Status:

Hi Geoff

That's old stuff. You'd be amazed at some of the wierdy things people are
doing with Linux - after all, how many OSs are there out there with free
source code?

Cheers
Steve


At 18:50 03/03/99 GMT, you wrote:
>Don't believe me?
>
>Doubting dogs. Put it in the news!
>
>See http://www.empeg.com/main.html
>
```

Right to reply

It's good practice with email to quote a message
that you are replying to – the person who sent you
the original message might not remember what the
message was about, for instance. In Eudora Light,
you can reply to a message by opening the message,
going to the Message menu and choosing 'Reply.'
You may want to edit huge messages you're replying
to, rather than quoting the whole thing again.

87

```
     To: bankmanager@bank.com
   From: Geoff Harris <geoffh@paragon.co.uk>
Subject: I want an overdraft
    Cc:
   Bcc:
X-Attachments:
─────────────────────────────────────────────
Hi dude

Listen man, I need some bread, and I need it bad. Leave some in my account and I'll stop hassling
you!
```

Be polite

While email is generally considered to be less formal
than conventional letter writing, you should always
consider who the message is for. If it's a business
email, for instance, it's unwise to begin the message
"Hi!" and resort to over-familiarity or slang. The
normal conventions of letter writing should still
apply.

postmaster

■ about us ■ spamming ■ login
■ network news ■ contacting us ■ register
■ faqs

● Will I be able to attach or receive documents with my e-mail messages? ▲

As long as your browser supports the attachment of documents and files, you are able to send documents. Attachments sent to you at your postmaster account appear as "hot-links" that can be downloaded and viewed. GIF and JPEG images are deciphered and displayed on your PC without having to launch a viewer application.

● Who should sign-up with postmaster? ▲

● Everyone should sign-up, especially in today's changing and fast-paced world
● People who are currently paying to have an e-mail account
● People who are currently sharing e-mail accounts
● People seeking a permanent e-mail address
● People without their own PC's but with access to the Web via various terminals available to them (Internet kiosks, universities, public access facilities, WebTV, etc)
● People who have e-mail accounts at work but feel that they cannot use the service for private correspondence
● People who regularly change their Internet Service Providers to take advantage of competitive pricing or promotional packages
● Mobile professionals
● Students and teachers
● Travellers

● Is it is easier to send e-mail to other postmaster users? ▲

Yes it is. To send an e-mail to another postmaster user, all you need to do is type their e-name - (i.e. send to "john", no need to type "john@postmaster.co.uk").

Web email attachments

Most Web-based email systems will now let you
attach files to your messages, in the same way as
conventional email systems. Sending larger
attachments (anything over 1Mb) this way can be
slow, however, so you may want to get a POP3 email
account, such as the free ones provided by
Freeserve, Virgin Net or Tesco Net, if you intend to
send large files to friends or colleagues.

89

Send To:	tpottery@aol.com		Copy To:

Subject: Here's a lovely picture of Gillian Anderson

Arial ▾ 10 ▾ **B** *I* U ...

Here she is!

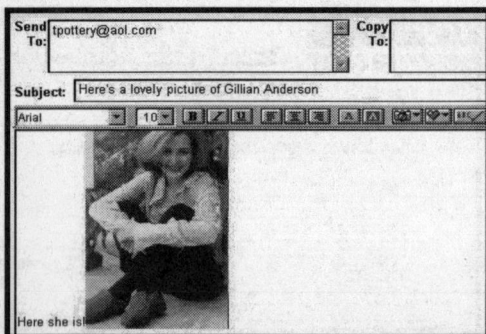

Beware AOL email pictures

With the latest version of AOL, you can embed pictures in your email or set an image as a background to your message. But remember that these design flourishes will only be appreciated by people who are also using the latest version of AOL, AOL 4.0i.

CHAPTER THREE

THE WORLD WIDE WEB

Everyone seems to have a Web site these days, so we've compiled some really useful tips for exploring the most exciting part of the Internet and using the most popular Web browser programs...

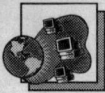

90

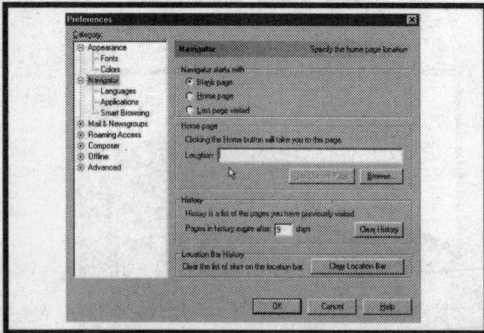

Why does my browser always go to the Netscape home page?

You can easily change the page your Web browser automatically opens. In Netscape Navigator, go to the 'Edit' menu, then 'Preferences' and click on the 'Navigator' category. Select the Home Page option in the 'Navigator starts with' section. Because browser authors are guaranteed lots of page hits if their software always goes to the company's site first. But you can change it to something more useful, like a Web search site or the weather report. Simply add the address and hit 'OK.'

91

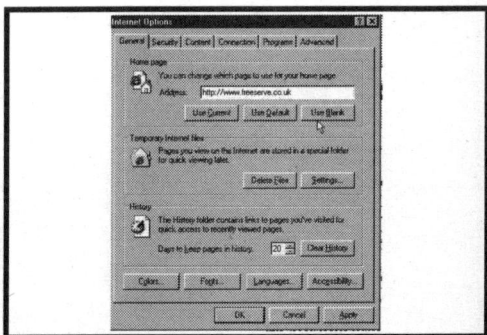

Why does my browser always go to the Microsoft home page?

It's the same principle with Microsoft Web browsers. In Internet Explorer 4, you can set the page you want to be your default (again, a news or search engine page is a good choice). Go to the 'View' menu and select 'Internet Options.' You can then set a new Web page as the starter page, or click 'Blank' to prevent any Web page from loading. Having to wait for the Microsoft page each time does get tiresome.

92

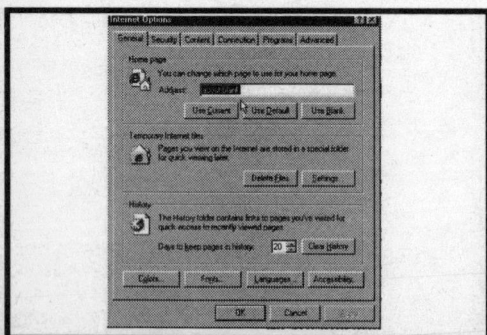

Why does my browser always go to the Freeserve home page?

Every time you open the Freeserve copy of IE4 it will try to connect you to the Freeserve Web site, and other ISPs set up IE so it keeps going to their site, too. This can be a pain if you just want to open up the browser without going online to change the preferences, for instance. To change this 'start' page, open IE4 and go to the 'View' menu. Then choose Internet Options. Click 'Use Blank' and you will stop IE4 from trying to load Freeserve's (or whoever's) site each time.

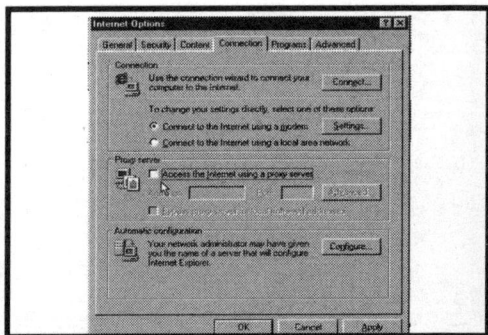

Web browsing problems with Freeserve

If the Freeserve IE4, won't let you open Web sites when you're connected to another ISP, go to the View menu, and select Internet Options. Pick the Connection tab. Half way down you will notice a box called 'Access the Internet using a proxy server.' If you are going to be using it with another ISP, untick this box. When you want to go back to using IE with Freeserve, tick it again. The proxy server settings speed up the retrieval of popular Web sites, but it only works when you're connected to Freeserve.

94

How can I save a whole Web site to my PC?

It's easiest to get a program called an offline browser. We like WebWhacker, available from http://www.bluesquirrel.com/, and MemoWeb 98, from http://www.goto.fr/. Trial versions of both are available from the Web sites. You can save text and pictures from Web sites quite easily. If you want to save text from a site, go to the 'File' menu of your Web browser, select 'Save as' and then choose 'text.' If you want to save a picture, simply right-click on it and follow the save options.

95

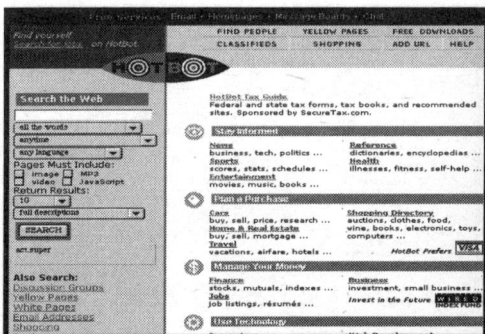

How do I find the Web sites I want?

Although there are millions of pages, it's not as difficult as you might think thanks to special software called 'search engines' that can take you to the exact sites you want. You must make your searches as specific as possible, however. One of the best search engines is HotBot, at http://www.hotbot.com/. HotBot has more Web sites stored in its database than any other search engine

96

Look at AltaVista

Another good search engine is AltaVista
(http://www.altavista.com). It is very good at letting
you specify your search with more accuracy. You can
enter phrases in double quotes "like this" for an
exact match, you can use the plus sign (+) to make
sure a word is included and you can use the minus
sign (-) to exclude words from your search.

97

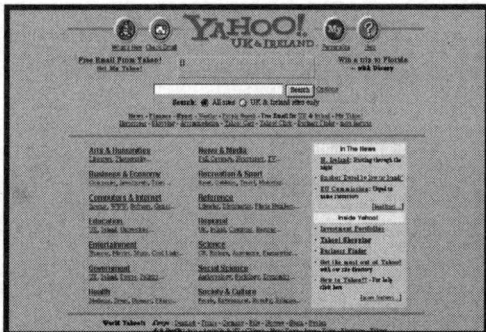

Use search directories

If you want to do a quick search on a specific subject – a band or movie, for example – try a beginner-friendly directory service such as UKplus (http://www.ukplus.co.uk) or Yahoo! (http://www.yahoo.co.uk). Both have huge directories of sites on popular topics, or link with search engines for more complex searches. They also filter out loads of American results.

98

Don't forget Portals

Many big Internet companies, such as Netscape
(http://home.netscape.com/uk) and Freeserve
(http://www.freeserve.net), have turned their Web
sites into 'portal' sites. As their name suggests, these
portal sites act as gateways to interesting content on
the Net, and list quality Web sites under easy-to-find
categories – sport, weather, kids, and so on. Many
portals sites offer extra services such as beginner's
Internet guides and free Web email addresses.

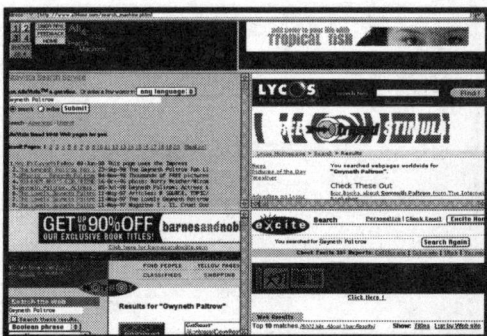

Use Meta searchers

As an alternative to conventional search engines and portal sites, try using a metacrawler to find Web sites of interest – simply a search site which runs your query through several search engines at once and then collates the results in a logical, orderly fashion. Our favourite meta searcher is Metacrawler (http://www.metacrawler.com), but you also get good results with SavvySearch (http://guaraldi.cs.colostate.edu:2000) and All4One (http://www.all4one.com).

100

Ask Jeeves

Another beginner friendly search site is the oddly named Ask Jeeves at http://www.aj.com/. You simply enter a question in normal English, such as "how do I grow Bonsai?" and wait for Ask Jeeves to come back with the results from various search engines. You can also see what kind of questions other Internet users are asking – as you'd expect, they range from the sublime to the ridiculous.

101

Do the Yell

BT's directory enquiries service is rather expensive at over 40p per call. It's much cheaper to log onto the Web and connect to the Electronic Yellow Pages at http://www.yell.co.uk/ or the renamed FreePages service – now called Scoot – at http:/www.scoot.co.uk/ Both services are fast and excellent, and cheaper than directory enquiries.

102

Main Page • Products • Filtering • Submit/Search
Free Trial • Support • News • International • Map

Cyber Patrol Filtering Technology

for HOME

for EDUCATION

for BUSINESS

At the heart of Cyber Patrol's top-rated Internet filtering software product family are its high performance filter engine and its world-renowned CyberNOT™ and CyberYES™ Lists. The filter engine is optimized for speed, employing proprietary technology and encrypted files. The CyberNOT List identifies researched sites and resources that contain material that may be found to be objectionable according to a set of clearly defined criteria. The CyberYES List highlights student-friendly, educational sites for ages 6-16.

Find Out More!

- CyberNOT™ List Overview
- CyberNOT™ List Criteria
- The CyberNOT™ Oversight Committee
- The CyberNOT™ Search Engine
- The CyberYES™ List
- Submit-a-site to the CyberNOT™ or CyberYES™ Lists

How do I block Web pornography?

You can install Net filtering or censoring software to stop kids finding porn site. As well as preventing access to specific sites they can provide password access to programs, log PC activity and react differently with different users. There are quite a few products available, among which CyberPatrol, at http://www.cyberpatrol.com, stands out, though it can intimidate beginners. The safest approach is to supervise your kids as they use your computer, or keep it in a family room with adults around.

103

Netscape NetWatch

NetWatch is Netscape Navigator's built-in ratings protection feature. It lets you control what kind of web pages can be viewed on your computer.

Click to set up NetWatch

PICS Ratings Standard

NetWatch uses an Internet rating standard known as PICS - the Platform for Internet Content Selection. PICS is designed to help parents, teachers, and employers screen out material they feel is inappropriate for children or employees. PICS gives web publishers a standard way to describe the content of web pages; it gives browsers like Navigator a standard way to read the description.

NetWatch recognizes two independent PICS-compliant ratings systems, RSAC and SafeSurf. Each system employs a different method to describe in as much detail as possible the levels of potentially offensive content on web pages.

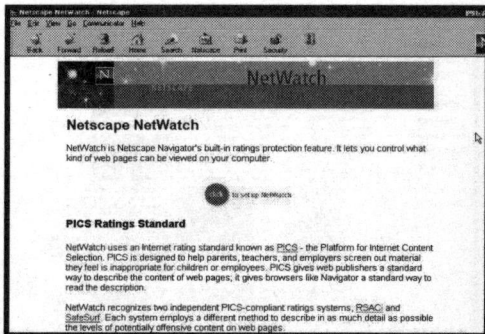

Filtering with Netscape

There is also a good filtering tool available with Netscape Communicator 4.51, on our CD – go to the Help menu of Netscape, and select 'Net Watch.' You can then set up NetWatch to block Web sites according to sexual content and other criteria. If you subscribe to AOL, check out the company's Parental Controls, which control email, the Web, newsgroups, chat rooms and more. It's more beginner friendly than CyberPatrol, though arguably less effective.

104

Tate Collections

Home
Collections
Galleries
What's On
Information
Mail Order
Supporters
Visitors Book
Site Guide

The Tate holds the national collections of British Art and of international modern art. You can now browse the General Collection which includes all works in the collection with the exception of works on paper in the Turner Bequest. The Great Collection and New Acquisitions are also available.

Currently, around 6000 works are illustrated – this number will continue to increase as we scan more images. Some images cannot be shown for copyright reasons, but we are working actively to develop new agreements with copyright holders.

The collection of historic British art ranges from the sixteenth century to the present day. Highlights include major works by Hogarth, Gainsborough, Reynolds, Stubbs, Wright of Derby, Blake, Palmer, Constable, the Pre-Raphaelites, Whistler, and Sargent. Home to the Turner Bequest, the Gallery holds the largest collection of paintings, drawings and watercolours by JMW Turner.

The collection of international modern art features important works by artists such as Picasso, Matisse, Duchamp, Epstein, Spencer, Mondrian, Gabo, Nicholson, Hepworth, Moore, Magritte, Dali, Giacometti, Schwitter, Bacon, Pollock, Rothko, Warhol and Beuys. The collection also includes works in all media by leading contemporary artists in Britain and from around the world, for example, Freud, Richter, Hamilton, Horn, Hirst and Whiteread.

Displays of the collection change regularly, and works are also loaned or sent on tour. Check the latest displays here in the Galleries section if you are planning a visit.

The Tate Gallery Library, Archive and Study Room contain material

Can I re-use material from Web sites?

Not without the permission of the authors. All original or legally republished material is automatically protected by international copyright agreements. Using it without permission makes you a criminal. Would you want people re-using your hard work on their own Web pages?

Finding free software on the Web

There are lots of Web sites containing free or cheap software for you to download. The best places organise software in categories. Of these, the most complete is Jumbo at http://www.jumbo.com. You should also check out Tucows at http://www.tucows.com and DaveCentral at http://www.davecentral.com/. Most software companies are on the Web, and nearly all offer free software utilities, add-ons for software and trial versions.

106

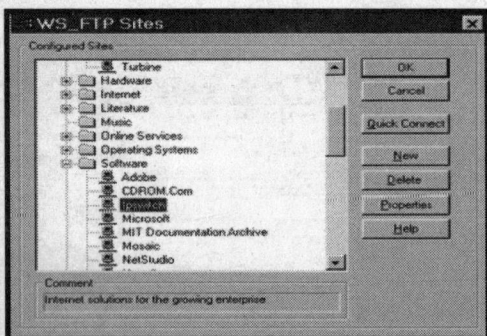

Go direct to the FTP site

When you download files from the Internet using your Web browser, you may notice that the address reads ftp://company.com/file.xxx instead of the more usual http:// company.com/file.xxx. This is because the file is being downloaded from an FTP server instead of a Web server. While your browser can happily cope with this if the files are relatively small, if a file is more than a couple of megabytes in size you're better off downloading it using a dedicated FTP program – they're usually faster and more efficient. Make a note of the address (URL) of the file and enter it into your FTP program to start the download.

107

Category:
- Appearance
  - Fonts
  - Colors
- Navigator
  - Languages
  - Applications
  - Smart Browsing™
- Mail & Groups
- Composer
- Offline
- Advanced

Advanced   Change preferences that affect the entire product.

☒ Automatically load images and other data types
   (Otherwise, click the Images button to load when needed)
☒ Enable Java
☒ Enable JavaScript
☒ Enable style sheets
☒ Enable Autoinstall
☐ Send email address as anonymous FTP password

Cookies
◉ Accept all cookies
○ Accept only cookies that get sent back to the originating server
○ Do not accept cookies

☐ Warn me before accepting a cookie

[Help] [Cancel] [OK]

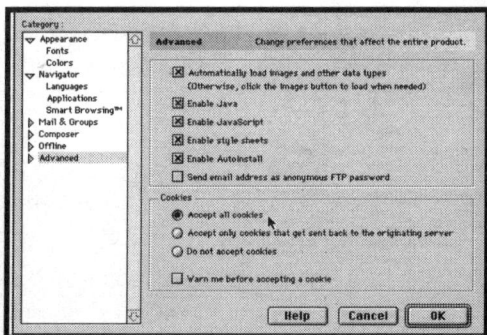

What are cookies?

There is nothing sinister about cookies, and they
are NOT computer viruses. A cookie is similar to a
saved computer game. It records your progress
through a Web site and stores this information on
your hard disk. The next time you visit that Web site,
it is set up according to your cookie. Cookies can be
deleted, but you will lose the information they
contain, so the next time you visit that Web site, it
will be as if you've never been there before.

108

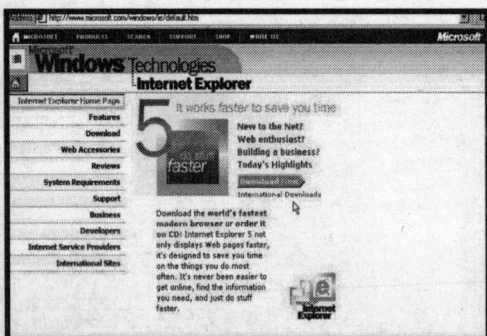

Internet Explorer tips: installation

Microsoft's Internet Explorer (IE) is an excellent Web browser 'suite' that also includes programs for sending email, visiting newsgroups and making a Web site. It's best to install Internet Explorer 4 (or 5) from our cover CD, otherwise you'll run up big phone bills downloading this bulky program from the Microsoft Web site (http://www.microsoft.com/ie/).

109

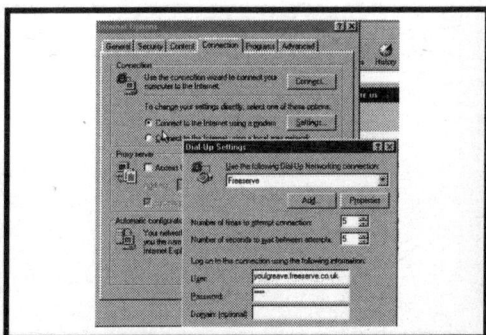

Internet Explorer tips: auto connect

IE can automatically connect to the Web when you want to visit a site. Simply go to the 'Internet Options' under the 'View' menu and click the 'Connection' tab. Click the button 'Connect to the Internet using a modem' and then 'Settings.' You should see your service provider listed, along with the password. Click 'OK.' Next time you open IE, enter a Web address and hit Return, you should automatically connect to the Web via your ISP (if your modem's on!)

110

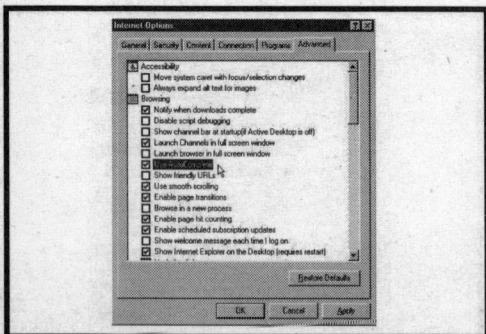

Internet Explorer tips: visiting sites

When you want to go to a Web site, you enter the address in the long white bar near the top of the IE screen and hit return (or use keyboard combination CTRL L). But you don't need to keep typing in laborious Web addresses this way. You can always miss off the 'http://' bit, for example, but IE4 also has an 'auto complete' feature that remembers the addresses of sites you've been to before and automatically completes them. This feature is turned on and off by going to the program's View menu, then Internet Options. Click the 'Advanced' tab, and the Auto Complete tick box is the seventh one down.

111

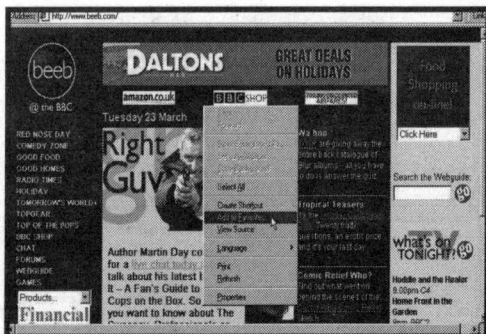

Internet Explorer tips: saving sites 1

When you come across a site you really like, you can save it for future reference, turning it into what IE calls a 'Favorite.' Saving sites this way means they're always at hand. Here we are at the Beeb site at http://www.beeb.com. Looks good, so to save it for future reference right-click anywhere on the site and choose 'Add to Favourites.'

112

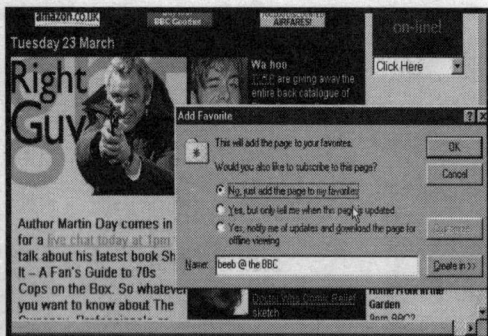

Internet Explorer tips: saving sites 2

In the next box select 'No, just add the page to my Favorites' and click 'OK.' If you click the box called Create In, you can add the site to a folder, or create a new folder for it. This is neater than having lots of individual pages sitting there loose.

113

Internet Explorer tips: saving sites 3

Now go to the Favorites menu, and you'll see the Beeb site, saved for future reference – note the folders we referred to in the previous step. If you are pushed for time, you can store a link to a page in the Favorites menu without actually visiting the page. Right click on a link to a page, then select the 'Add to Favorites' command in the pop-up.

114

Photo: Katerina Jebb

Internet Explorer tips: saving pictures

You can save any image on a Web site onto your hard drive, or as a desktop pattern on your PC – for some reason best known to Microsoft, these patterns are known as 'wallpaper.' Simply right-click on the image and choose 'Set as Wallpaper' (there's a similar function in Netscape Navigator). Or just save the picture for future reference.

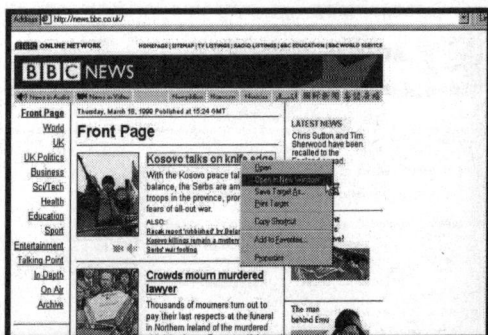

Internet Explorer tips: following links

Sometimes you may want to follow a link on a page but keep the current page in the browser window. You can open a link in a new browser window by right-clicking on it and selecting the 'Open in New Window' command. A second IE window opens with the new page within it.

116

```
System  [≡] http://www.microsoft.com/ie/ie40/download/cd/iechanml.htm

Microsoft®
Internet Explorer 4.0
Update Channel

Welcome to the Internet Explorer Update Channel!
Use the Internet Explorer Update Channel to download the latest version of Internet Explorer either now or at a
later time if that's more convenient.

        You have version:   Internet Explorer 4.01 with SP1

        You have the latest version available

Installing Internet Explorer 4.0 Suite Components and Add-Ons
Internet Explorer offers a host of components and add-ons to enhance your Internet experience. To add
components that you didn't include when you originally downloaded Internet Explorer 4.0, go to the Internet
Explorer Components Download page (Windows 95, Windows NT). You can access the component download page
at any time by choosing Product Updates on the your Internet Explorer Help menu.

▲ Back to the top

© 1998 Microsoft Corporation. All rights reserved. Terms of Use.
Photo Credits: PhotoDisc
```

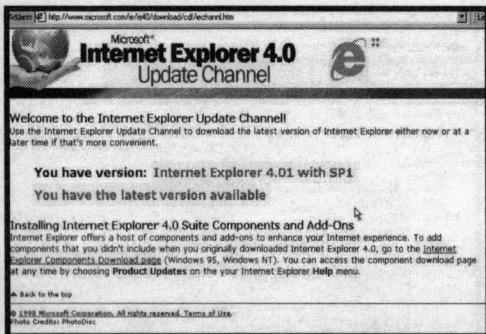

Internet Explorer tips: updating

You can add new components of IE4 as they appear
by downloading them from the Microsoft Web site.
Updates and software fixes ('patches') are also
available at regular intervals. You can check if your
version of IE4 is the latest by going to the Favorites
menu and selecting Microsoft Internet Explorer in
the Software updates folder. This takes you to the
Microsoft Web site's IE update channel, where your
version is checked and you're told if there are any
newer versions that are available.

117

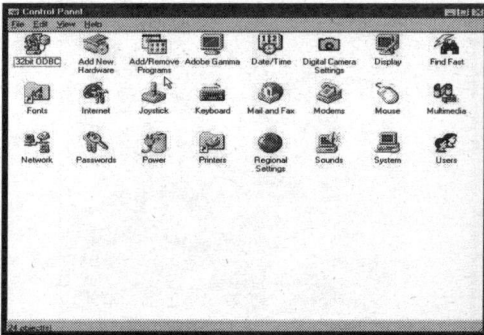

Internet Explorer tips: installing

Once you have Internet Explorer 4 or 5 on your computer (it's pre-installed with Windows 98) NEVER install IE3 over them without first removing IE4 or IE5 using the Add/Remove Programs Control Panel in Windows. Just slapping an earlier version of IE over a later version can mess up your copy of Windows, forcing a complete re-install – it really is that serious.

118

Internet Properties

| General | Security | Content | Connection | Programs | Advanced |

Home page
You can change which page to use for your home page.

Address: about:blank

Use Current | Use Default | Use Blank

Temporary Internet files
Pages you view on the Internet are stored in a special folder for quick viewing later.

Delete Files | Settings...

History
The History folder contains links to pages you've visited for quick access to recently viewed pages.

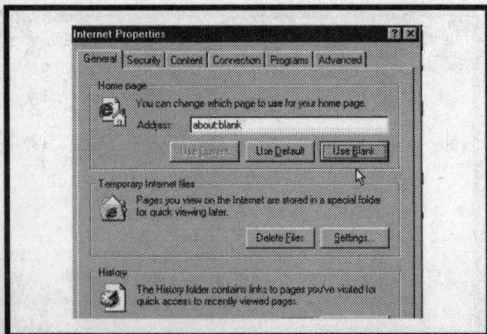

Internet Explorer tips – viewing files

If you want to use IE to view files on your hard drive or on a CD, and you don't want to connect to the Internet when you open the browser, change the default home page. Open the Internet Control Panel and select the General tab. Click on the Use Blank button in the Home page box. The next time you open IE4, you'll find it presents you with a blank page.

119

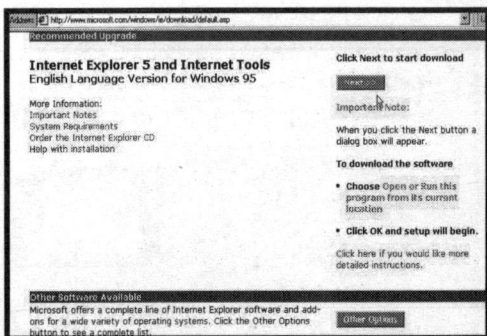

Internet Explorer tips – upgrading

If you're using IE4 and want to update to IE5, all you have to do is install IE4. All your files and settings will be updated to the new version of the software. So there is no need to completely uninstall IE first if you are simply upgrading to a more recent version. Doing so may wipe out all your preferences, such as saved sites ('Favorites').

120

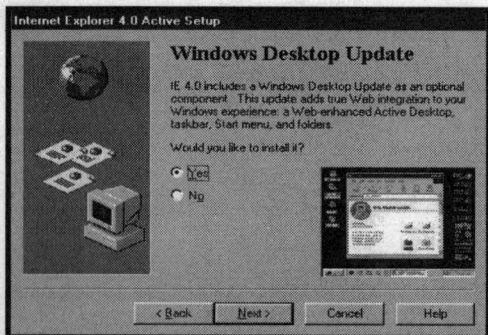

Internet Explorer tips – Desktop Update

When you are installing IE4 – from the CD of an ISP such as Freeserve, for instance – don't install the Windows 95 Desktop Update component unless you really can't live without it. It can slow down older PCs, and changes the way Windows 95 looks and feels – IE takes over your Windows desktop, turning it into a glorified Web browser. Note that this feature is automatically there in Windows 98, though you can turn it off.

121

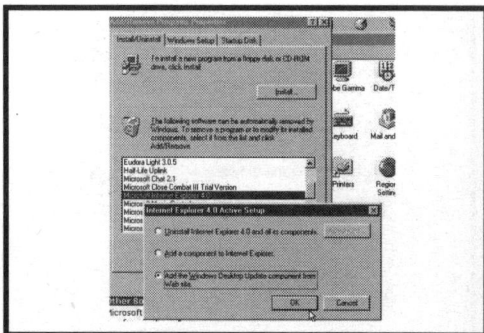

Internet Explorer tips – removing Desktop Update

Even if you have clicked to install the Desktop Update, don't despair – you can easily remove it. To get rid of the Desktop Update component, open the Add/Remove Programs Control Panel and select Microsoft Internet Explorer 4.0 in the list, then click on the Add/Remove button. In the Internet Explorer 4.0 Active Setup window, select the Uninstall Windows Desktop Update option and click on the OK button.

122

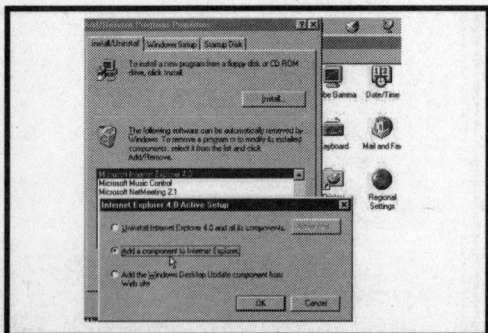

Internet Explorer tips – adding components

If you want to add an extra component to IE4, open the Add/Remove Programs Control Panel and select Microsoft Internet Explorer 4.0 in the list, then click on the Add/Remove button. In the Internet Explorer 4.0 Active Setup window, select the Install component option and click on the OK button. This takes you to the Web site where you can choose the components you want to add.

123

```
Settings                                          ? X
     Check for newer versions of stored pages:
       • Every visit to the page
       ○ Every time you start Internet Explorer
       ○ Never
   Temporary Internet files folder
   Current folder:   C:\WINDOWS\Temporary Internet Files

   Amount of disk space to use:
   ─────┬──────────────────────   60.2MB (3% of drive)

   Move Folder...    View Files...    View Objects...

                              OK          Cancel
```

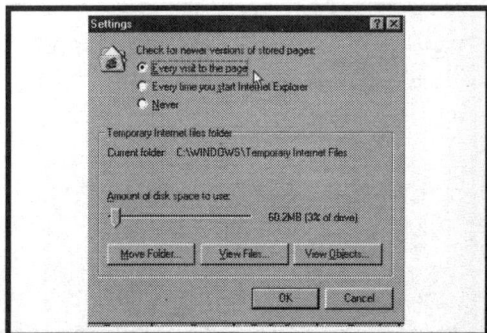

Internet Explorer tips – speeding it up

If you want to make sure IE is running as fast as it should be, make sure the program isn't updating all of the pages stored in its cache every time you connect to the Internet. Open the Internet Control Panel and select the General tab. Click on the Settings button in the Temporary Internet files area. In the Settings window, select the 'Every visit to the page' option.

124

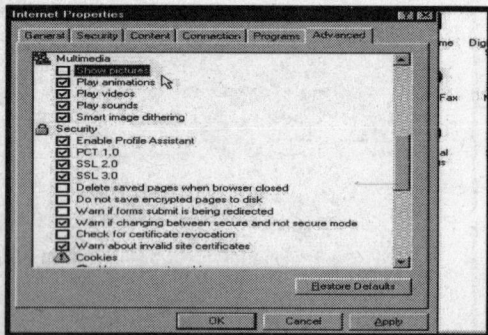

Internet Explorer tips – turning off images

If a Web site is taking ages to load, or if you've got a slow modem (28.8kbps or less), turning off the pictures on Web sites will speed things up. This is useful if you only want to download a program from a Web site, or extract a bit of information. Go to the 'View' menu, 'Internet Options,' then pick the 'Advanced' tab. You can turn pictures, sounds and video on and off via the Multimedia section.

125

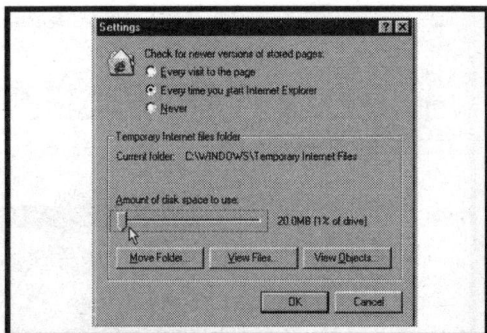

Internet Explorer tips – temporary files

Every time you visit a Web site with IE4, it stores lots of temporary files to ensure you can retrieve the site quickly when you return to it. In the same Settings dialog box as mentioned in tip 116, make sure IE4 doesn't use too much disk space for temporary files by reducing the space used to 1% of your hard drive using the slider. Then click OK.

126

BBC News | Sci/Tech | Opposition grows to web caching ban - Mic

| File | Edit | View | Go | Favorites | Help |

Toolbars ▶
✓ Status Bar
Explorer Bar ▶

Back ... esh Home Search Fav

Address 🗃 /sci/tech/newsid. 298000/298498

Fonts ▶ Largest
Larger
Stop Esc ✓ Medium
Refresh F5 Smaller
Smallest ⬉

Source
Full Screen F11 Universal Alphabet (UTF-8)
User Defined
Internet Options... ✓ Western Alphabet

caching of copyright

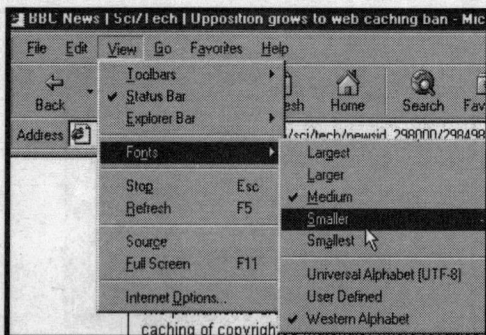

Internet Explorer tips – appearance

For some reason known only to the programmers of Internet Explorer, the browser displays Web pages using quite large fonts. This can make the text on some pages look bigger than intended. Select the Fonts icon in the IE4 toolbar and select Smaller or Smallest. This will make the Web page look more like the site designer wanted it to.

127

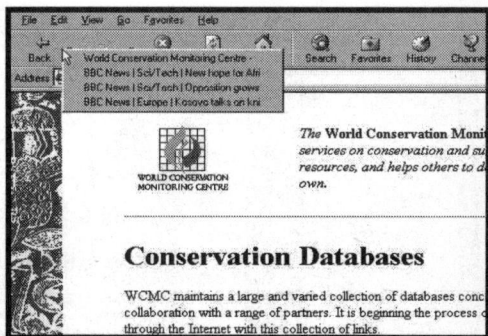

Internet Explorer tips – navigation

If you've visited a lot of Web pages in a session and want to go back to an earlier site, you can click the Back button until you reach the page you want. Next to the Back button is a small black arrow – click on it an a menu listing all the pages in the current session is displayed. Select the page you want to return to by clicking the name in the list.

128

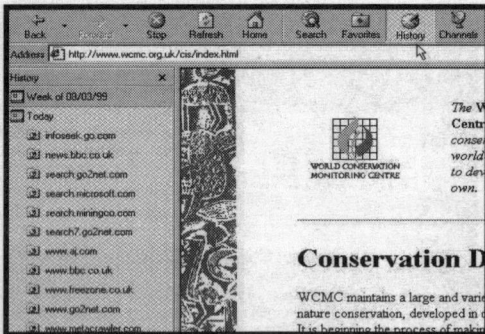

Internet Explorer tips – offline browsing

You can return to Web sites without being connected to the Net (and running up phone bills) by clicking the History icon (a sundial) on the toolbar. It displays all the Web sites you've visited recently, in neat chronological order. Select Work Offline in the File menu and you can open these sites. To specify how far back the History function goes, simply select 'Internet Options' from the View menu. The new version of IE, IE5, makes offline browsing even easier. See page 70 in the magazine.

129

Internet Properties

General | Security | Content | Connection | Programs | **Advanced**

- Accessibility
  - ☐ Move system caret with focus/selection changes
  - ☐ Always expand alt text for images
- Browsing
  - ☑ Notify when downloads complete
  - ☐ Disable script debugging
  - ☐ Show channel bar at startup(if Active Desktop is off)
  - ☑ Launch Channels in full screen window
  - ☐ Launch browser in full screen window
  - ☑ Use AutoComplete
  - ☐ Show friendly URLs
  - ☑ Use smooth scrolling
  - ☑ Enable page transitions
  - ☑ Browse in a new process
  - ☑ Enable page counting
  - ☑ Enable scheduled subscription updates

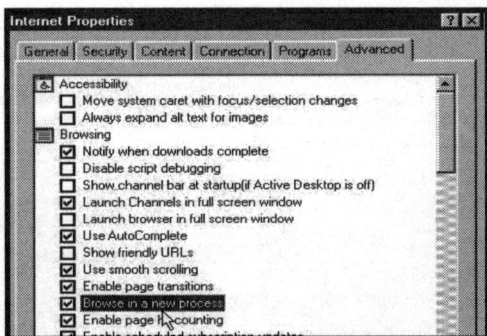

Internet Explorer tips – stability

You can make the program a little more stable by opening the Internet Control Panel and selecting the Advanced tab. Scroll down the list and select the 'Browse in a new process' option. This gives IE4 its own chunk of memory and makes it less likely to crash your PC if IE4 crashes. Thankfully, this is quite a rare event, as IE is already a highly reliable program.

130

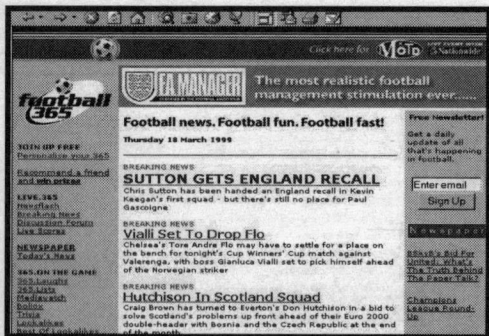

Internet Explorer tips – viewing fullscreen

To see a packed Web page in its full glory, click on the Fullscreen icon (next to the little icon of the radio telescope). This allows you to see much more of the Web site which is obviously useful if you have a small monitor (15-inch or below). Simply click the icon again to return the display to normal.

131

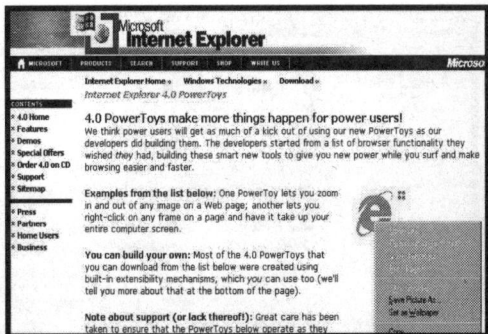

Internet Explorer tips – get the Power Toys

Install the Internet Explorer Power Toys, on our CD. They let you zoom in and out of Web pages with a mouse click and use your favourite search engines straight from the address bar. You can also switch images on and off via the image toggler button and open frames in new windows by right clicking and select a menu option. Right-clicking on keywords on a Web page automatically searches for related pages.

132

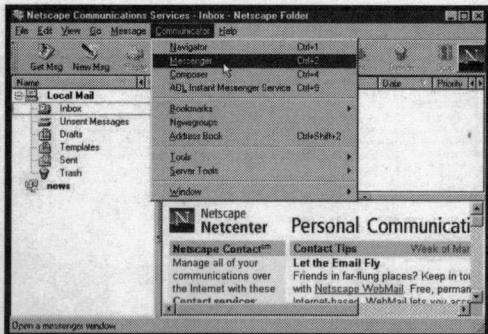

Netscape tips – installation

An excellent alternative to IE4 is Netscape Communicator. Install Netscape Communicator 4 (on our disc), not the standalone version of Netscape Navigator 4. Unlike earlier versions of the browser, Netscape Navigator 4 does not have the ability to send email messages by clicking on an email link on a Web page. This can be very annoying if you want to send a quick message to a company who's site you've found on the Web. Many forms also submit content by email, and these forms just won't work in Netscape Navigator 4.

133

ymbol ◯ Name

NEWS.com

olbrooke Warns Milosevic

asoline Prices Soar

ustralians Save 47 Beached

olphins

evorkian to Represent

Read Newsgroups

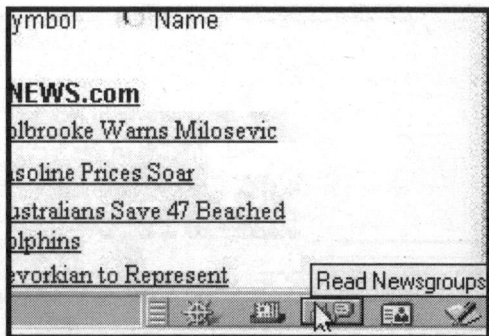

Netscape tips – the elements

Trying to find the different parts of Netscape Communicator can be confusing. On the bottom right of the Netscape application window, you'll notice a little bar which contains icons for Web browsing, sending email, joining newsgroups and making your own Web page. Click on the horizontal lines on the left of the bar and it pop ups, giving you easy access to the icons.

134

Preferences

Category
- Appearance
  - Fonts
  - Colors
- Navigator
  - Languages
  - Applications
  - Smart Browsing
- Mail & Newsgroups
- Roaming Access
- Composer
- Offline
- Advanced

Navigator   Specify the home page location

Navigator starts with:
- ◯ Blank page
- ◯ Home page
- ◯ Last page visited

Home page
Clicking the Home button will take you to this page.

Location: http://www.paragon.co.uk

[Use Current Page] [Browse...]

History
History is a list of the pages you have previously visited.
Pages in history expire after: 9 days   [Clear History]

Location Bar History
Clear the list of sites on the location bar   [Clear Location Bar]

[OK] [Cancel] [Help]

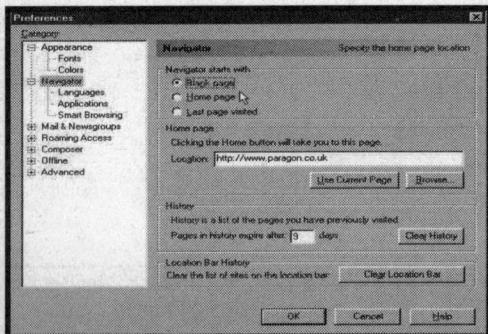

Netscape tips – start page

If you get tired of seeing the same old Web site
when you start up Navigator, you can start up with a
blank page. Select the 'Preferences' command in the
'Edit' menu and then click the Navigator category.
Then tell Navigator to start with a blank page.

135

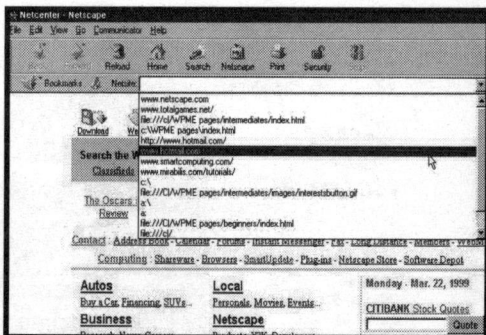

Netscape tips – efficient navigation

As with IE, Navigator makes it easy for you to revisit sites you've been to during a Web session. While you can obviously use the Back and Forward arrows to navigate, you can also get a drop-down list of recently visited sites by clicking and holding the Back and Forward arrows. The Go menu contains a similar list, and another one appears when you click the black arrow at the end of the address bar.

136

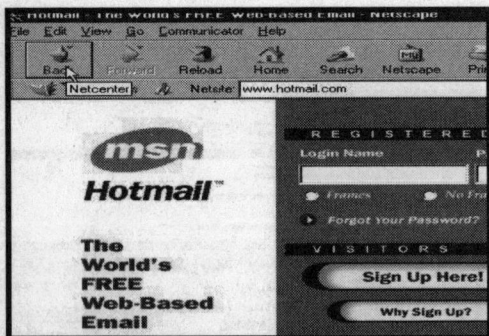

Netscape tips – going back and forth

Here's another neat trick. Simply hold the cursor over the Back or Forward arrows and up pops the title of the Web page which you would have visited if you'd have clicked the button. It lets you see exactly where you're going, which can save time and hassle.

137

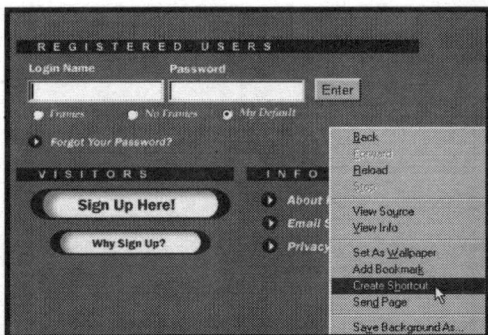

Netscape tips – right mouse-clicking

As with IE4, the right mouse button is useful with Navigator. Right-click on a link on a Web page, for example, and you can get the program to open the link in a new window. Also, you can right-click anywhere on a Web site and get the program to create a shortcut that appears on your desktop. Click on the shortcut and Navigator opens the site (IE has a similar feature).

138

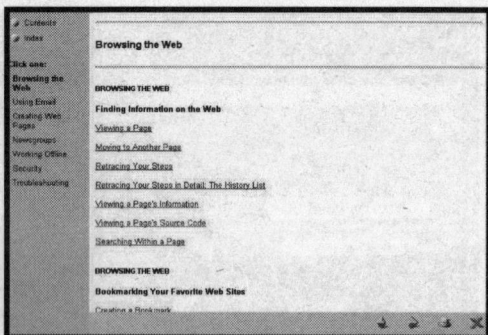

Netscape tips – getting Help

There's an excellent help section in Netscape Communicator. Go to the 'Help' menu, then 'Help Content' and a separate window appears with extensive information about all the programs in Communicator, Navigator included. Very impressive.

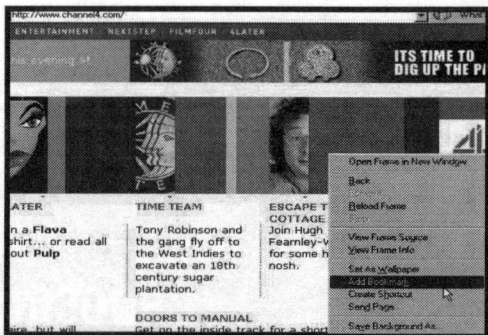

Netscape tips – saving sites

Sites you wish to save for future reference are called 'Bookmarks' in Netscape Navigator. As with IE, you can right-click on a favoured site to save it as a Bookmark, and it will appear under the Bookmark menu, either loose or in a folder. You can create folders for your Bookmarks by clicking New Folder in the Bookmarks menu.

140

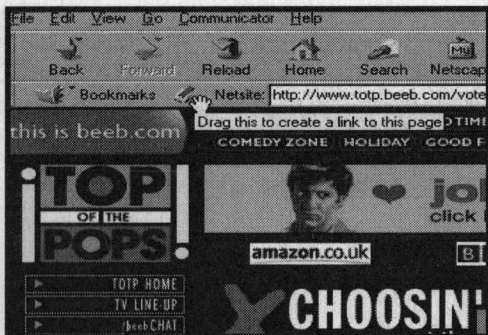

Netscape tips – dragging links

You can also drag a Web site link into your Bookmarks collection. When the site is open, click on the little icon next to 'Netsite' (the address bar) and you can drag the address of the currently open Web site into the Bookmark folder or other folders on the Netscape Navigator interface. Above, we are dragging the Top of the Pops Web site over to our Bookmarks folder to save it for posterity.

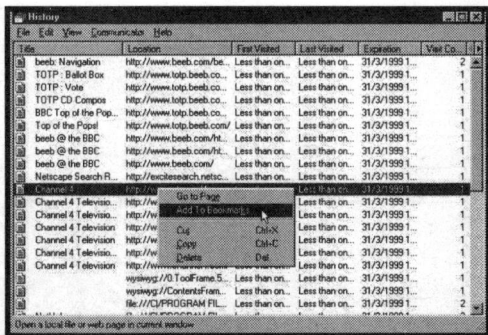

Netscape tips – retrieving sites

If you forget to Bookmark a site a while ago, you may be able to retrieve it from Netscape's History function. Simply hit the keyboard combination CTRL H (APPLE H on Macs) to see an archive of recently visited Web pages. If a site is in the History, you can right-click it and add it to your Bookmarks.

142

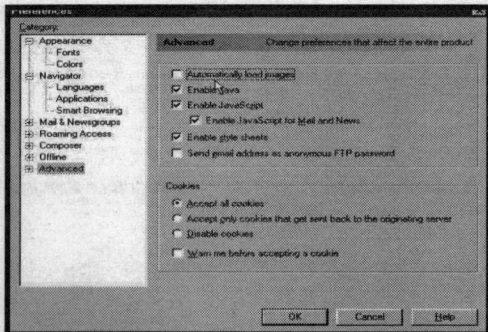

Netscape tips – speeding it up 1

As with IE4, you can turn off pictures in Web sites so they download faster. Go to the 'Edit' menu, then 'Preferences,' then 'Advanced.' Unclick the box called 'Automatically Load Images.' If you want to see one particular image while the rest are still turned off, just right-click its 'place holder' and choose 'Show Image.'

143

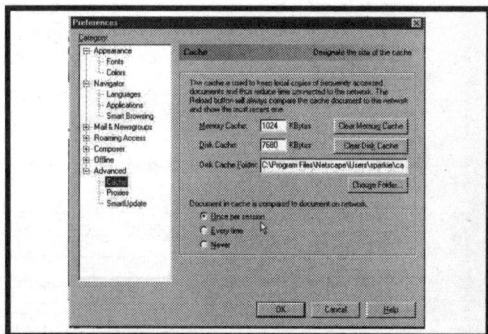

Netscape tips – speeding it up 2

To stop Navigator from wasting time by checking its cache too often, go to the 'Edit' menu and select 'Preferences,' then 'Advanced.' Next, click the plus sign (a triangle on Macs) and then click 'Cache.' Under 'Document in cache is compared to document on network,' check the 'Once Per Session' option. You can also reduce the size of the cache here, to save hard disk space.

144

Netscape tips – printing with frames

Say you want to print a Web page, but it uses 'frames' and gives you a confused print-out. Click once in the frame you want to print to make it the active frame on the page. Now click the Print icon or select the Print Frame command in the File menu and your frame is printed by itself.

145

ParkerNet
http://parkernet.com/

Welcome to ParkerNet

Welcome to ParkerNet, the only Web page design agency and Internet consultancy based in Portishead, England.

Many small, local businesses are missing out on the advantages that can be gained by having a page on the Internet. Apart from anything else, a small site consisting of just a few Web pages can act as a great advertisment for your services - even if you don't have an Internet connection at your business.

All you need to have on your Web page is a phone and a fax number. customers to contact you by email, then that can be set up too. Parke process the email and forward it to you as a fax message.

Contact details

If you already have an email account of your own, you can send me ar clicking on this link clive@parkernet.com
If you are in the UK, you can phone 07050 092 969 during normal business hours.

Open Frame in New Window
Back
Reload Frame
Stop
View Frame Source
View Frame Info
Add Bookmark
Send Page

Netscape tips – print from new windows

Alternatively, you can right-click somewhere in the frame window and select the Open Frame in New Window command. When the new window opens, you can print it, save it to disk or bookmark it.

146

Netscape tips – storing email addresses

You can drag links from Web pages directly onto the Personal Toolbar or into folders you have added to the Personal Toolbar. This is a great way of storing email addresses. If you don't want to open your email program you can select an email link from the Personal Toolbar and send mail from within Communicator.

147

ADVERTISING LICENSING	SERVICES CAREERS	MAGAZINES BOOKS	SUBSCRIPTIONS PRESS OFFICE		CONTACTS WEBSITES
a Bedford	Ad Sales		Junior Ad Executive	223	emmab@paragon.co.uk
r Bedford	Finance		Finance Director	234	treverb@paragon.co.uk
Beedles	Circulation		Subscriptions Assistant	200	jbeedles@paragon.co.u
rrine Blackman	International		Account Executive	205	cathb@paragon.co.uk
h Bousadda	PowerStation		Staff Writer	284	adamb@paragon.co.uk
Borrows	Circulation		Subscriptions Asst.	200	subs@paragon.co.uk
an Butt	Console		Editorial Director	228	gecko@paragon.co.uk
Butt	Play		Editor	263	ryan@paragon.co.uk
ca Casal	Marketing		Marketing Manager	225	monica@paragon.co.uk
e Chai	Accounts		Management Accountant	227	jackie@paragon.co.uk
Cleall	Ad Sales		Group Ad Manager	213	peterc@paragon.co.uk
	Information				

Netscape tips – become a keyboard king

Netscape Communicator has a host of keyboard shortcuts to make it faster to use. Avoid the time-wasting tedium of pointing the mouse at a link and clicking on it by pressing the Tab key instead. As you press the key, each link on the page is highlighted in turn. Press the Enter key to follow the link.

148

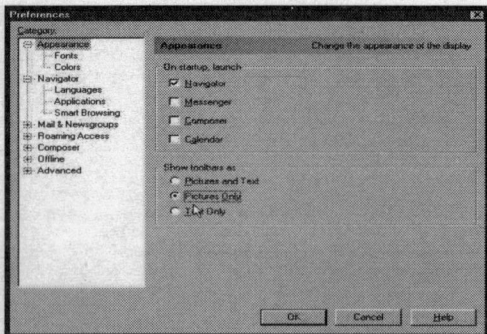

Netscape tips – make more room

If you only have a small monitor, you can get rid of the status bar across the bottom of the browser window by pressing Control Alt S. Pressing the same combination returns the status bar.

To create more space to view Web pages, select the Preferences command in the Edit menu and then select the Appearance category. In the 'Show toolbar as' section, select Pictures Only to get rid of the text under the icons in the main toolbar.

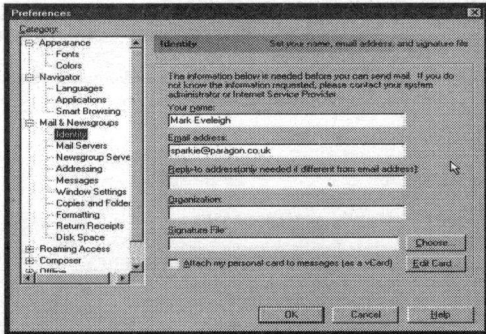

Netscape tips – add your identity

Add your identity to Netscape Communicator. You must make sure that your name and email address has been entered into the Preferences, for example, so you can send and receive messages. Go to the Preferences command in the Edit menu then select the Mail & Groups/Identity category. Enter your name, email address and other details into the boxes.

150

The Oscars in Review

Netscape Career Center
Find the job that CLICKS

Click here!

Contact : Address Book - Calendar - Forums - Instant Messenger - Fax - Lo
Computing : Shareware - Browsers - SmartUpdate - Plug-ins - Netsc

Autos
Buy a Car, Financing, SUVs...

Business
Research, News, Careers...

Computing & Internet
Free Software, News, Shops...

Education
Colleges, Financial Aid, K-12...

Entertainment
Movies, Music, TV, Oscars!...

Local
Personals, Movies, Events...

Netscape
Products, Y2K, Developers...

News
Oscars!, Tech, Weather...

Personal Finance
Investing, Portfolio, Taxes...

Real Estate
Find a House, Remodel...

Netscape tips – check for updates

Remember to regularly check for updates to Communicator. You can do this by visiting the SmartUpdate pages at http://home.netscape.com/download/ su1.html. Alternatively, you can check by clicking on the NetCenter link found in your Bookmarks, or via the Start menu.

CHAPTER FOUR

NEWSGROUPS

Newsgroups (collectively known as 'Usenet') are regarded as the last bastion of the original, text-based Internet which was established in 1969. Usenet is a huge number of discussion groups (over 30,000 at the last count) each devoted to a specific subject. Messages sent, or 'posted,' to each group can be read by anyone in the world who subscribes to that particular group.

151

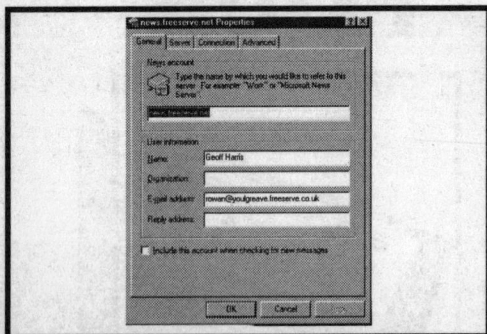

Where can I get a list of all newsgroups?

You can't. ISPs carry only a few of the 60,000 or more newsgroups in existence. Reasons for not carrying a group include: it's private, it's moribund, it's in a language you can't display, it's only of local interest or it contains material illegal in certain countries because of sexual, political or religious content. Your newsreader program can only download a list of groups supplied by your ISP from its news server.

152

Address http://www.dejanews.com/[ST_rn=qs]/qs.xp?QRY=PlayStation&OP=dnquery.xp&ST=QS&DBS=2

Search Results   help

Messages 1-25 of exactly 13681 matches for search PlayStation:
Find books on playstation at computerliteracy.com
and get $10 off through March 28!

h for
beanie

	Date	Scr	Subject	Forum	Author
1.	99/03/22	028	Compro Playstation	it.annunci.varie	Cristiano Orazi
2.	99/03/22	027	Re: Looking to buy broken pl	rec.games.video.sony	TGreen8272
3.	99/03/22	027	NEED PLAYSTATION	alt.games.sony-playst	White Tiger
4.	99/03/22	027	[ACH] Playstation PATCHER	fr.petites-annonces.i	Kline
5.	99/03/22	027	VENDO GAME ENHANCER e ACCESS	it.annunci.usato.info	OSCAR DALVIT
6.	99/03/22	027	VENDO GAME ENHANCER PER PLAY	it.annunci.usato.info	OSCAR DALVIT
7.	99/03/22	027	[RMI] COMPRO Playstation	it.comp.console.plays	Mauro Cerboni
8.	99/03/21	027	Playstation Accessories - ww	alt.bbs.ads	PSX Depot
9.	99/03/21	027	Re: Dreamcast Better than Pl	rec.games.video.sega	XXirkoU
10.	99/03/21	027	Playstation Website	alt.games.video.sony-	Tim
11.	99/03/21	027	Playstation Website	alt.games.video.sony-	Tim
12.	99/03/21	027	Compro Playstation	it.comp.giochi	Cristiano Orazi
13.	99/03/21	027	Compro Playstation	it.comp.giochi.action	Cristiano Orazi
14.	99/03/21	027	Compro Playstation	it.comp.giochi.annunc	Cristiano Orazi
15.	99/03/21	027	Compro Playstation	it.comp.giochi.rpg	Cristiano Orazi
16.	99/03/21	027	Compro Playstation	it.comp.giochi.sporti	Cristiano Orazi
17.	99/03/21	027	Compro Playstation	it.comp.giochi.strate	Cristiano Orazi

When newsgroup messages disappear

With over 500Mb of new newsgroup messages
(postings) generated by Net users every day the old
is dumped to make way for it. In fact, it isn't unusual
to find replies to dumped questions – extremely
confusing for infrequent visitors. ISPs keep
newsgroup postings for anything from a day to a
week depending on their resources. If you want to
search older material try DejaNews at
http://www.dejanews.com/. This a Web site where
you can access an archive of newsgroup postings.

153

How do I send to newsgroups anonymously?

Use software called an 'anonymous remailer.' These are automated systems that strip out the header showing who and where you are and send the message on to the address you specify. Check with your remailer of choice for details and guarantees. You can find a good Web site on the subject at http://world.std.com/~franl/crypto/remailers.html/.

154

Address http://www.freeserve.co.uk/support/status.htm

~~details will not be obliged to mind ponies in accordance~~
with the relevant sections of the AUP.
We hope users agree that this policy will help us to
maintain a high quality of service for all our customers.

· · · · · · · · · · · · · · · · ·

The following message was posted to freeserve.announce
on 10.01.99:

On Monday 11th January maintainance of the news service
will be carried out between 0615 and 0730 and news will be
unavailable for about 20 to 30 minutes during this interval.

The work is part of the continuing process of upgrades in
performance and reliability to the Freeserve service.

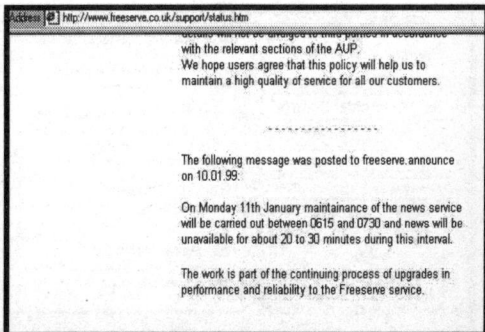

Why can't I get some listed newsgroups?

Probably because since you last downloaded the list
from your ISP it decided to stop carrying that group
– many ISPs do this if there are no postings to a
group for a week or two. Download a new list and
check. If it's there and you still can't get it you need
to phone or email the ISP. There may be a problem
with its news server, as happened with Freeserve in
the screenshot above.

155

Newsgroups

Parental Control

About Parental Control

Chat	Newsgroups
Downloading	Premium Games
Email	Screen Names
iMs	World Wide Web

Go to Newsgroup Controls

AOL's Newsgroup Controls provide the following features for parents who wish to restrict their children's use of newsgroups:

1) BLOCK EXPERT ADD OF NEWSGROUPS: Prevents your child reading any newsgroups for which he/she knows the Internet-style newsgroup name (e.g. "alt.games.quake").

2) BLOCK ALL NEWSGROUPS: Prevents your child from accessing *any* newsgroups.

3) BLOCK BINARY DOWNLOADS: Prevents your child downloading binary files (games, pictures, software, etc.) from any newsgroup.

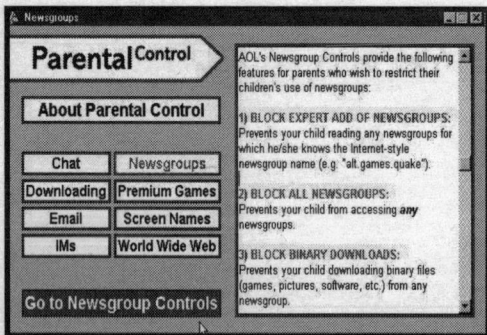

Watch what your kids are accessing

Newsgroups, alas, are a major source of online pornography. Many of the groups under the 'alt' (alternative) hierarchy are sex-related, and pornographic pictures (binaries) can be easily exchanged. If you don't want your kids to access dirty newsgroups, good ISPs to use are Freeserve and LineOne, which are both family and friendly, and AOL. AOL offers parental controls for newsgroups.

156

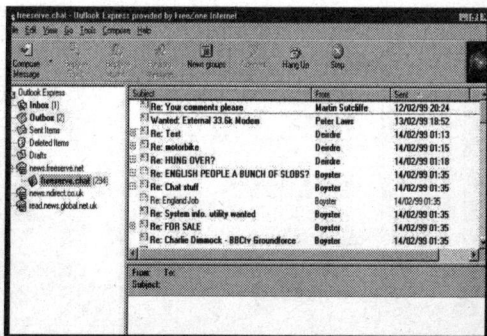

Use the right tools

The easiest way to read newsgroups is to use the
newsgroup programs in your Web browser –
Netscape Messenger, which is part of Netscape
Communicator, or Outlook Express, part of Internet
Explorer. Note that not all service providers supply
access to all of the newsgroups. In general, UK-
based service providers will supply access to all of
the English-language newsgroups. Some newsgroups
that the service provider deems unsuitable may not
be available, usually those with explicit sexual
content.

157

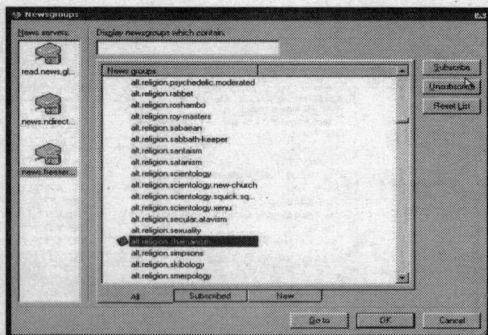

Subscribe swiftly

Because there are so many newsgroups, it's common
practice to 'subscribe' to newsgroups you are
interested in. Your newsreading program will then
give you quick access to these specific groups from
the bewildering collection of 20,000-plus groups
usually carried by your service provider. In Outlook
Express, you can quickly find newsgroups on your
interests by entering the subject in the box labelled
'Display newsgroups which contain.'

158

```
Re: Idiot                                          _ □ ×
File  Edit  View  Tools  Compose  Help
  ⊟ ⊜  ✕  ✂ ⓒ ⓒ  ⊕ ⓒ ⓒ  ◆ ◆

     From:  gburnore@databasix.com
     Date:  19 March 1999 08:26
Newsgroups:  alt.flame.alt.usenet.kooks
   Subject:  Re: Idiot

In alt usenet kooks - <36F1B859.72F5C8F7@home.com>, Odious
<Odious@home.com> wrote:
: youjustdontgetit@you.dolt wrote:
: >
:
: In to the kill file with your child molesting hubby, fat ass.
Another fat joke. Typical.

: Plonk
```

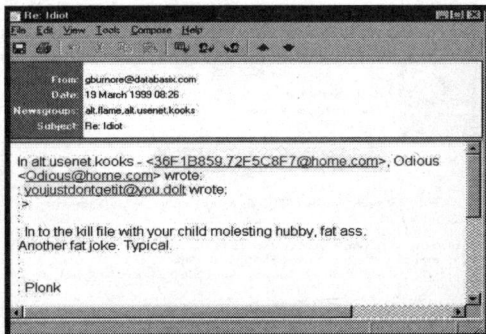

Put out the flamers

If you upset someone in a newsgroup, they might
send you abusive email, an activity known as
flaming. An easy way to dodge flame mail is to alter
the settings of your newsreader program, whether
it's Outlook Express, Netscape Communicator or
FreeAgent, so you have a false name and email
address. If you are anonymous, you won't get the
fallout.

159

PLAYSTATION FOR SALE

File Edit View Tools Compose Help

Reply to Author

From: Lisa
Date: 15 March 1999 15:43
Newsgroups: uk.games.video.playstation.forsale
Subject: PLAYSTATION FOR SALE

Dual Shock Playstation for sale.
Modified and has 9 games inc. Tomb Raider 3, Spyro the Dragon,
Michael Owens
WLS99, Toca2, Formula 1 98,Colin Mcrae Rally, V Rally, Ridge
Racer 4, And
Critical Depth.
All except for Critical Depth are Back ups.
Includes 2 controllers, 1 Dual Shock 1 Normal.
1 Memory Card, all in mint condition with original packaging, still
under
guarantee by Sony, and the people who modified it.

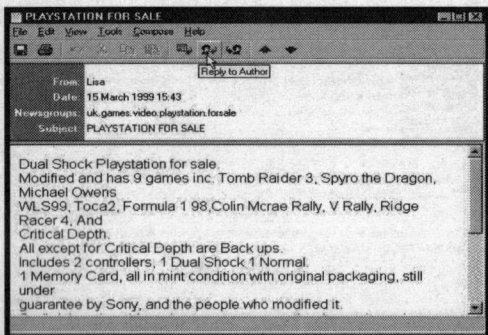

Answer by email

If you want to correspond with someone on a
newsgroup, do so by email. When you reply to a
message in a newsgroup, you have a choice of
posting a message in the group where everyone can
see it, or sending a personal reply direct by email.
This is recommended if you're sending someone
your personal details such as your phone number or
postal address. Guard your privacy online.

160

From: Jim Marshall
Date: 09 March 1999 00:24
Newsgroups: [alt.quit.smoking.support]
Subject: my six month anniversary....

This my first posting here, and is a newsgroup I should have searched out six months ago.

Saturday is my sixth month anniversary (as if you haven't figured it out), and haven't felt so good since I was about 13 or so (when I started smoking). It was perhaps the hardest thing I've ever done in my life, and anpathsis totally with anyone quitting.

What I have yet to be able to find much info on, are the effects on the human body. We all here about weight gain (I went from 140 to 170 pounds, and don't look skinny in more), but I have experienced several other effects personally, including:

    . enhancement of oratory and taste senses.
    . clearer complexion with less natural oils in both hair and in the skin.
    . increased energy.
    . decreased sexual desire (not impotence)
    . insomnia and/or the need of prolonged sleep.

Don't be put off!

While you need to take a few precautions with Usenet, don't be deterred from trying newsgroups out. Getting involved in a newsgroup discussion about a topic you are familiar with can be very enjoyable or helpful in times of stress (above). Being able to discuss your subject with people all over the world is very satisfying, especially if you can share the fruits of your knowledge!

161

From: Randy Pals
Date: 07 March 1999 14:04
Newsgroups: rec.martial-arts,rec.answers,news.answers,rec.martial-arts.moderated
Subject: rec.martial-arts FAQ part 1 of 4 [LONG]

```
        Topics Contained in this FAQ
        ================ == ==== ===

Part 1 of 4

  1) Introduction.

  2) What is a Martial Art?

  3) What kind of Martial Arts are there?  (the descriptions of
     various arts are in section 16, which is in parts 2 and 3.)

  4) Which Martial Art should I study?

  5) How do I choose a School?

  6) (a) This guy says that his style will make a Full Certified
         Warrior & Killer out of me in 3 months- is it serious?

     (b) What do I do to become the deadliest person in the world ?
```

Ask for help

If you're new to newsgroups in general, or just to a specific newsgroup, don't be afraid to ask. Post a message on the group containing your question and you'll get loads of helpful replies. You may get a few less than helpful replies too, but these are from old bores less tolerant of 'newbies' invading their space. To avoid this, make sure you check out the FAQ file on the newsgroup. A FAQ is a list of frequently asked questions and their replies. If you can't see a FAQ among the messages in the group, post a message asking where it is.

162

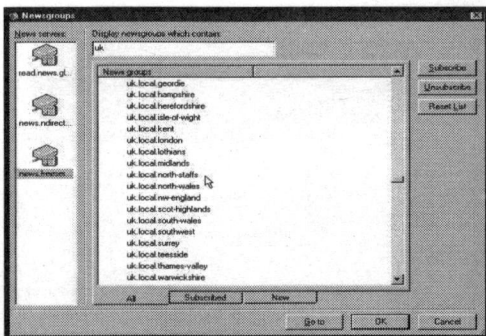

Fly the flag

Usenet can appear very US-dominated, but don't
forget that there are a couple of hundred UK-based
newsgroups as diverse as uk.food+drink.archives,
uk.media.tv.friends or uk.rec.pets.misc. Scroll down
the list of newsgroups supported by your service
provider until you find interesting-sounding ones
with the uk. prefix.

163

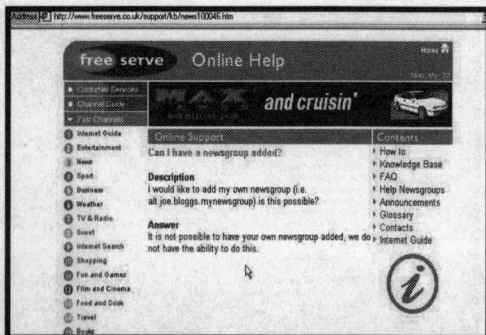

Get missing groups

If a newsgroup that you know exists isn't carried by
your service provider, there are a couple of options
available to you. The first is to send an email to
technical support requesting that the newsgroup is
added to the feed. As long as the group doesn't
carry dodgy content, there's no reason why the
service provider shouldn't add it to its newsfeed.
Second, you can access Usenet archives on the World
Wide Web by going to http://www.dejanews.com/
Enter subjects you're interested in and relevant
newsgroup postings appear.

164

USENET FEATURES

Learn More About Usenet Features

Since 1995, RemarQ has been the leading Usenet Newshub in North America, Europe and Asia. We've established global newsfeeds and bandwidth connectivity with leading Usenet service providers including Sprint, UUNET, and MCI.

Our servers process over 50 million articles/emails and transfer over 2.0 terabytes of information per day. RemarQ hosts over 30,000 newsgroups and carries over 400 Gigabytes of news on-line.

The growth rate for Usenet activity has been 10-15% per month and our connectivity has grown by 1 T1 line per week. Learn more about our connectivity and Network Topology.

In addition to the most complete collection of Usenet newsgroups, RemarQ brings users up-to-the-minute headlines in the supernews.* hierarchy.

Quality

Be independent

If your service provider won't support your favourite groups, you should consider subscribing to an independent newsfeed such as Supernews Wren. For $90 a year (about £60) you can subscribe to the 30,000 plus newsgroups available from SuperNews. The SuperNews Web site is at http://www.supernews.com/

165

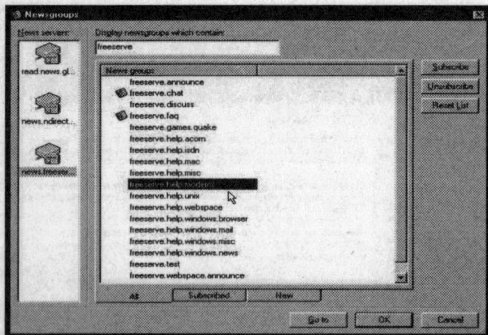

Save money on tech support

If you subscribe to one of the free ISPs, always check to see if there are any newsgroups on the company. These can be a rich source of technical information, saving you from having to phone up the pricey help lines. If you're with Freeserve, check out freeserve.help.misc, freeserve.help.modems and freeserve.faq. For a general, unbiased discussion of free ISPs, see alt.internet.providers.uk.free.

EXTRA!!

166

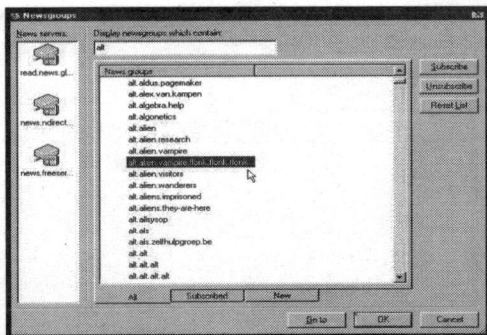

Subscribe sensibly

It's easy to get carried away with newsgroups and subscribe to loads and loads. Try to restrict yourself to the newgroups that you find genuinely interesting and useful. Avoid becoming swamped with useless information that just takes time to download. A lot of rubbish appears on newsgroups, and it has no place on your hard drive.

167

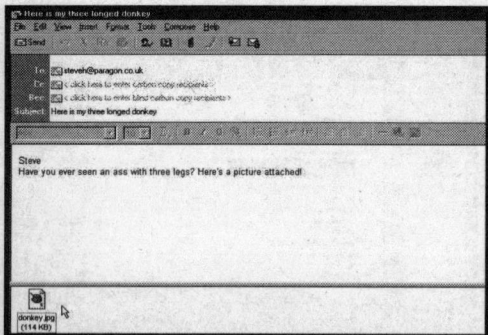

Keep the pictures out

It's best to treat newsgroups as a text-based discussion medium. Posting (sending) pictures to newsgroups slows the whole thing down for everyone. If you want to show the world your photos of three-legged donkeys, put them on a Web page and pass on the address to interested parties. Or compress them using WinZip or StuffIt and email them to your friends.

168

On 21 Mar 1999, Dr Ivan D Reid, muSR Facility wrote:

> In article <7d0r2v$754$1@newnews.global.net.uk>, al the pal wrote:
> >I have ordered a GSXR 600 (new one) but also for the same money is a P reg
> >750 this is a mint machine but has 5K on the clock.
>
> >What should I do stick with a new 600 with 2 years warranty and all that or
> >go for the 750 (may need a tyre soon).
>
> And inherit someone else's problems... Is insurance cost a factor?
> -- the 750 may be more expensive to insure than the 600. I presume it's
> also heavier on fuel, tyres and chains because of the increased power.

But the owner of the 750 will have suffered the worst of the depreciation
whereas you'll lose quite a bit off the value off of the 600 the moment
you ride it out of the showroom.

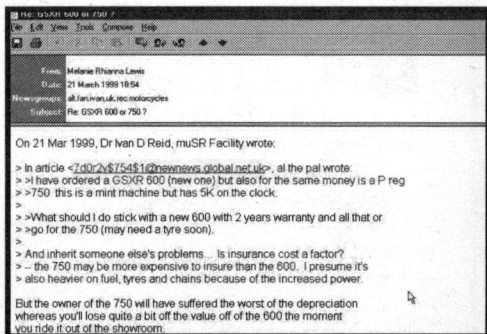

Quote quickly

If you reply to a newsgroup message, only quote the
bits of the message which are directly relevant. Most
newsgroup programs lets you quote the previous
message, putting a > character before the quoted
material. Simply highlight the unnecessary parts of
the quote and hit Delete on your keyboard. Never
quote reams of text, only to add "I agree"or
"rubbish!"

169

Consider mailing lists

Unfortunately, a lot of newsgroups are getting clogged up with junk messages (spam) or irrelevant postings from either a) lunatics b) drunks or c) boring US college kids and their mates. For more consistent and civilised discussion, consider joining a mailing lists – contributions are sent to you as email. Search for mailing lists on your interests at Liszt (http://www.liszt.com).

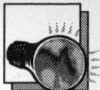

CHAPTER FIVE

MAKING A WEB SITE

Contrary to popular opinion, making your own Web site, or home page, is actually very easy. Web sites are built with a language of formatting commands, or tags, known as HTML (HyperText Markup Language). Sounds scary, but you can get programs which create all the HTML for you. Here's an easy guide to Web site creation.

170

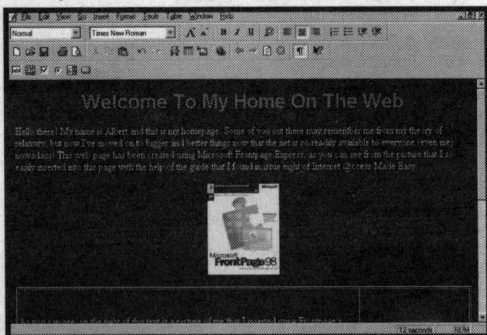

Start off with free programs

If you've never made a Web site before, start off with one of the free Web-site creation programs that come with your Web browser. These are Netscape Composer (part of Netscape Communicator) and FrontPage Express (part of Internet Explorer). You can then pay for a full commercial program, such as Adobe PageMill, if you need the extra power.

171

What's this site about?

So you want a Web site? What kind of Web site?
You must have a clear idea what kind of site you
wish to create. Most sites fall into five main
categories. Home pages include details of Internet
users, their family, friends and hobbies. Then there
are CV pages, club/association pages, pages put up
by specialists on certain subjects and business pages.
You must be clear from the outset what your site is
about. If you're vague, it will show.

172

These pages run in parallel

These pages run in series

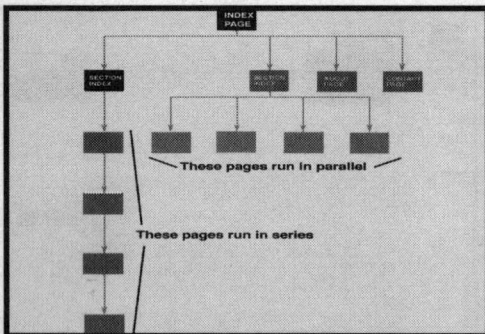

Plan, plan, plan

Once you have decided what your Web site will be about, you should start planning what sort of features and content it should include. It's best to start with a list of items – on a biography page, for instance, you could include a start page, a personal history, photographs, contact information and your hobbies. Drawing a flow chart will help.

173

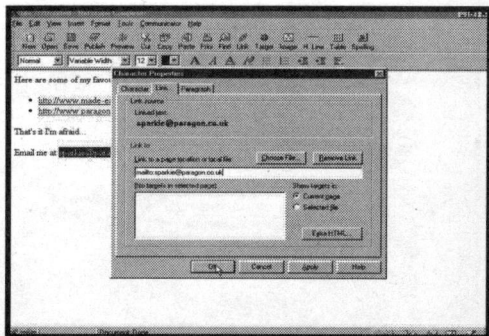

Don't forget an email link

Regardless of what kind of site you're making, you should always include contact details. A simple 'email me' link is enough, and will enable you to receive feedback, suggestions and general messages from a wide range of people. After all, the Internet is all about communication. Creating an email link in FrontPage Express and Composer is easy – highlight the text, click the icon of the anchor, and enter mailto: followed by an email address. See later in the book for detailed instructions.

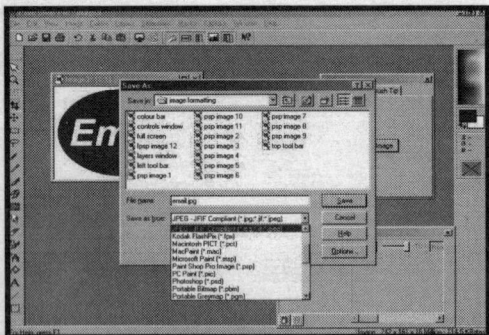

Getting your site online

Most home Internet users create Web sites on their
home PCs and then transfer ("upload") all the files
to the free Web space given by their ISP. Before
uploading the files that comprise your Web site, you
must get the file extensions right. These are .html
for HTML files, .gif for GIF image files and .jpg for
JPEG image files – pictures on Web sites are usually
JPEGs or GIFs.

Getting hold of graphics

Obviously, you will want to add your own text and
pictures to your Web site. The text you can type in
to the Web-site creation program, but how do you
add pictures to your site? The easiest way to add
photographs is to take them using a digital camera –
see the cover feature in the magazine. Or, you can
get them scanned in using a budget scanner, easily
found for under £100.

176

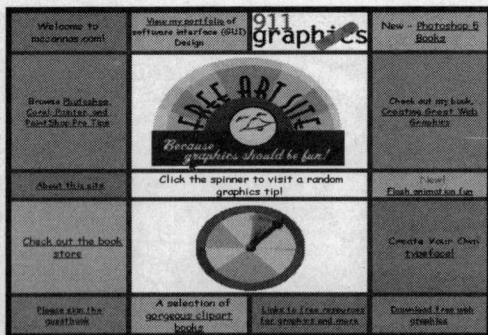

Getting graphics off the Net

If you are really stumped for pictures, you can get free graphics and even photographs off the Web, but they tend to look pretty cheesy. Better collections are Laurie McCanna's free graphics site at http://www.mccannas.com, or the Angelfire graphics library at http://www.angelfire.com/. For some invaluable tips on working with Web graphics and Web safe colours, see Lynda Weinman's site at http://www.lynda.com/.

Netscape Composer – starting a site

Composer, part of the Netscape Communicator suite on our CD, is the easiest Web-site creation program. To start a new Web page, click the 'New' icon on the toolbar. If it's an index or opening page for your Web site, you must name it index.html. This done, you can start typing in your text, which you can format with the word-processor style formatting commands.

178

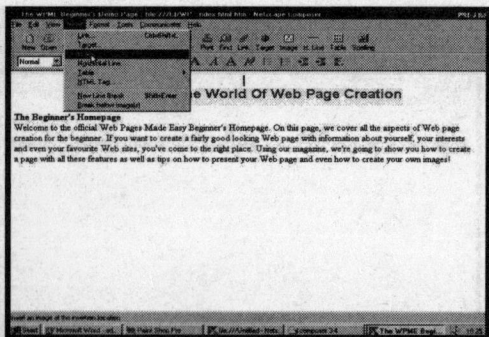

Netscape Composer – adding pictures

To add an image to your page, click on the 'Insert' menu at the top of the screen and select 'Image.' A window asks you to locate the image on your PC's hard disk or wherever. Your image should be saved as either JPEG or GIF, and should be as small as possible – big pictures take a long time for other Net users to download. Click OK to insert the image.

179

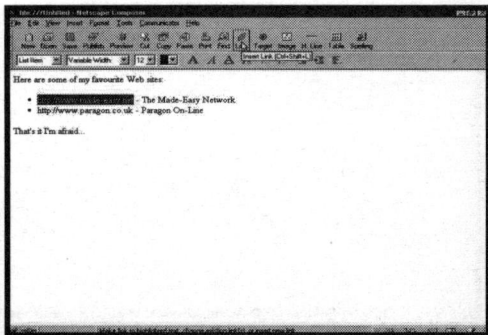

Netscape Composer – adding links

All Web sites should contain links, either to other Web sites or email addresses. It's this kind of interactivity that makes them interesting. If you want to turn a piece of text into a link to a Web address, highlight it and click on the 'Link' icon. To link to a Web site, enter the Web address; to link to an email address, type in mailto: followed by the address – yours, for example!

180

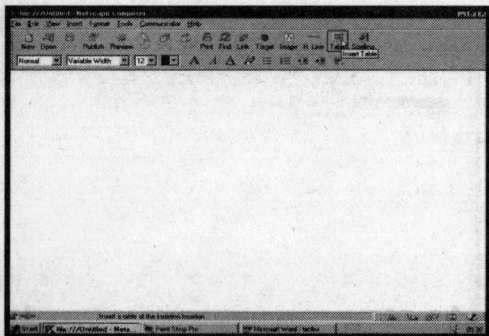

Netscape Composer – adding tables

Tables are another good way of breaking up information on your Web page, and it's easy to add them with Composer. Click the 'Table' tool located in the toolbar at the top of your screen. In the box that appears, specify the number of rows or columns. Left-click inside each of the cells to enter text. If you set the border size of the table to 0, the border becomes invisible.

181

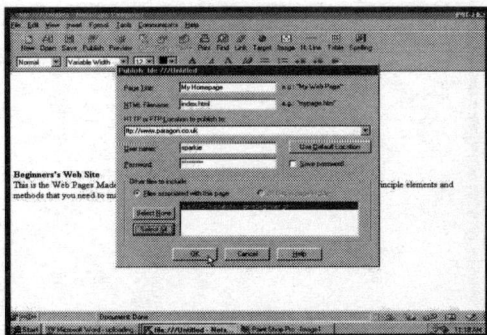

Netscape Composer – getting your site online

Save your site, making sure the first page is labelled index.html. Then, click the 'Publish' icon. Enter the username and password you use to connect to your ISP, and the address of your ISP's free Web space – call the help line if you don't know it. To get multiple files online, click 'Files associated with this page' to ensure everything gets copies over.

182

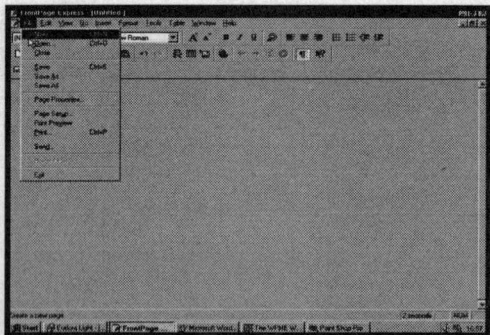

FrontPage Express – starting a site

FrontPage Express, part of Internet Explorer, is another easy site-creation program. To start a new page, click on the 'File' menu and select 'New.' You can then enter your text, formatting it as required – you can change the typeface, add colour, position the text left, right and centre, and pick a nice background colour. Be conservative when picking typefaces – it's best to use Arial, Courier or Times so all Net users can read them.

183

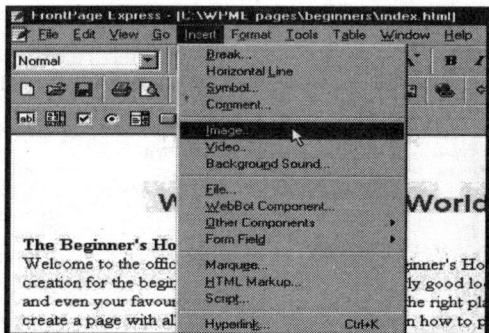

FrontPage Express – adding pictures

To add a picture to your new Web page, click on the 'Insert' menu and select 'Image.' A window appears where you can enter the location of the image or browse for it on your PC. To align the image, select one of the three justification tools on the toolbar left, right or centre. Right-clicking the image and picking 'Image Properties' lets you tweak the image.

184

```
FrontPage Express - [Untitled Normal Page]
File  Edit  View  Go  Insert  Format  Tools  Table  Window  Help

Bulleted List          Times New Roman        A  A   B  I  U

                                              Create or Edit Hyperlink
```

Here is a list of some of my favourite sites on the Web:

- http://www.made-easy.net - The Made-Easy Network
- http://www.paragon.co.uk - Paragon On-Line

Take a look, they're fantastic!

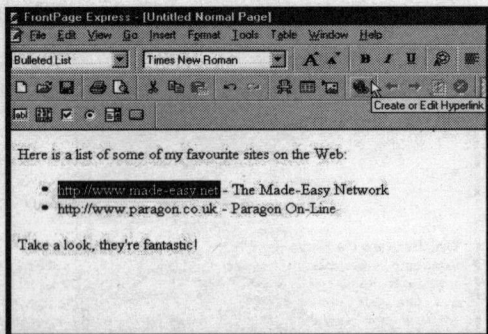

FrontPage Express – adding links

All Web sites should contain links, either to other
Web sites or email addresses. It's this kind of
interactivity that makes them interesting. If you
want to turn a piece of text into a link to a Web
address, highlight it and click on the 'Link' tool at
the top of the screen. Enter the site address and
click OK. To link to an email address, enter the email
address in the text bar and select 'mailto' from the
drop down menu.

185

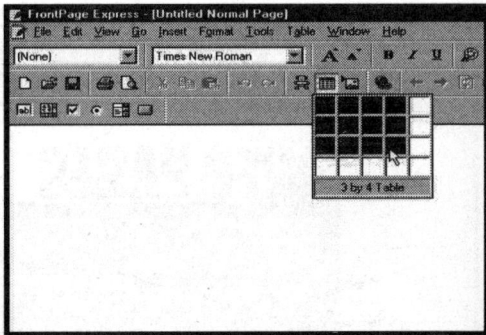

FrontPage Express – adding tables

Tables are another good way of breaking up information on your Web page, and it's easy to add them with FrontPage Express. Place your cursor where you want to add your table. Now, click the 'Insert Table' tool and drag the mouse across the number of cells that you want to include. Right-clicking the table and selecting 'Table Properties' lets you change its settings.

186

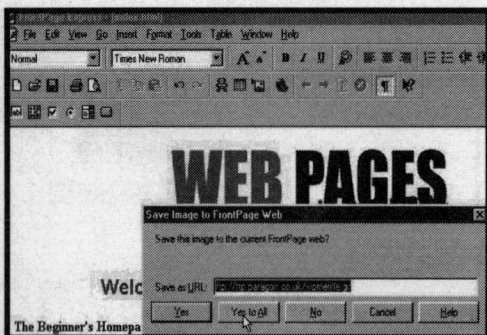

FrontPage Express – getting your site online

First save your site, by going to the File menu and Save As. Enter the destination and filenames of the pages on your hard drive, making sure you call the first page index.html. Then go to 'Save As' again and enter the FTP (file transfer protocol) of the Web space provided by your ISP – ask them if you are unsure – along with the filename of your Web page.

187

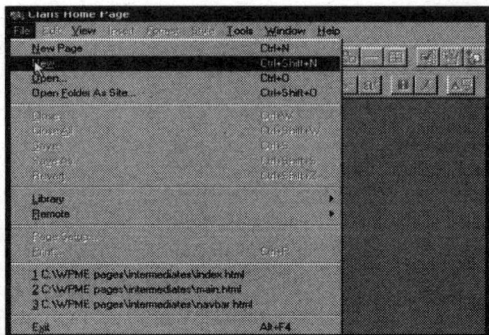

Claris HomePage – starting a site

If you are prepared to buy a site-creation program, a very easy one is Claris HomePage (http://www.filemaker.com/products/homepage3. html). To start off a new Web site in HomePage, click on the File menu and select 'New.' Don't just select 'New page' or click on the tool as this will only create a single page. You can now enter your text, as you would with a word processor.

188

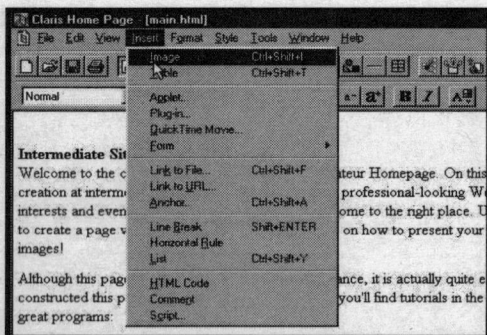

Claris Home Page – adding pictures

Move your cursor to where you want to include the image. Click on the 'Insert' menu and click on 'Image.' You will be asked to select the file that you wish to use. To change the image properties, right-click on the image and select 'Image Object Editor' from the pop-up menu which appears. Then edit the image as necessary.

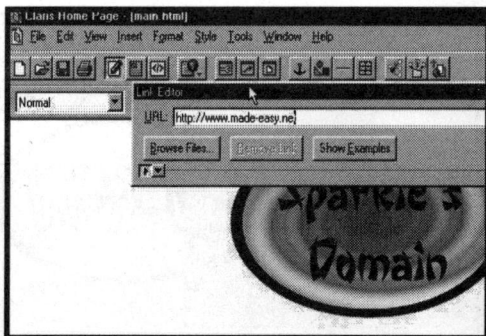

Claris Home Page – adding links

Highlight the text you want to turn into a link. Then click the 'Link Editor' icon. If you're linking to a Web site, enter the address in the white bar. If you're linking to an email address, enter mailto: in the white bar, followed by the email address. When the link is closed, a window will appear with the address in the 'to:' part.

190

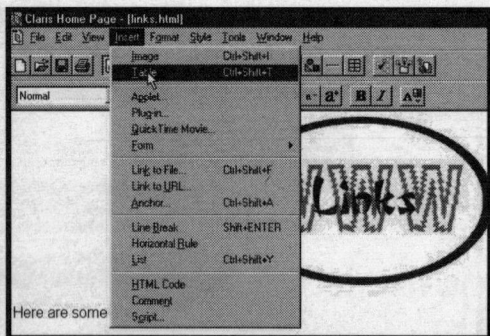

Claris Home Page – adding tables

To insert a table in Home Page, click on the 'Insert' menu and select 'Table' from the list of options that appears. In the following window, enter the number of table 'cells' that you want to create by giving the number of rows and columns in the table. When you've created your table and want to alter its properties, right-click on the table and select 'Table Object Editor.'

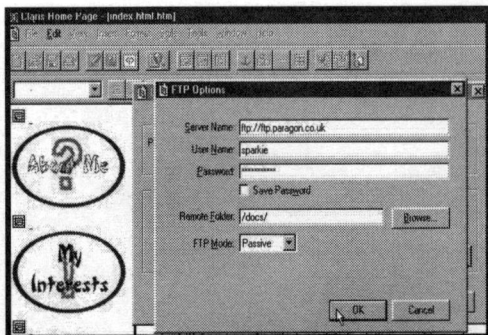

Claris Home Page – getting your site online

To copy your Web site to the free Web space provided by your ISP, click on the File menu and choose the 'Remote' option. Then, click on the 'Upload' option. In the window that appears, enter your page title and save your page. After a few other simple steps, you are asked to enter all your FTP details – call your ISP if you are unsure about them. Then click the 'upload' button.

192

```
Adobe PageMill
File  Edit  View  Search  Site  Help
  New Page    Ctrl+N
  Open...     Ctrl+O

  Print Setup...

  1 index
  2 hhh

  Exit
```

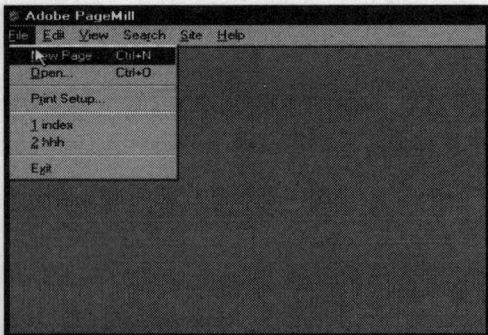

Adobe PageMill – starting a site

Page Mill is an equally powerful site creation program (download a trial version from http://www.adobe.co.uk). To start off, click on the File menu and then select 'New' using the left mouse button. You should then give your Web page an appropriate title by placing the cursor in the 'Title' text bar and typing in the name. You can then enter text in the main screen, formatting it as necessary by changing the font (typeface), changing the font colour, and increasing/decreasing the font size.

193

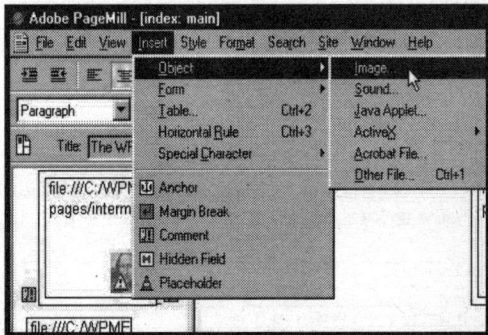

Adobe PageMill – adding pictures

Click on the Insert menu and then choose the 'Object' menu. Then, click on 'Image.' A window will appear which invites you to specify the location of the image that you want to insert. Click on 'Place' to insert it. To align your image, left-click on it to select it. Then, just click on one of the alignment tools at the top of the screen – left, right and centre.

194

- FileMaker Homepage 3.0
- Softquad HoTMetaL Pro 5.0
- Adobe PageMill 3.0
- PaintShop Pro 5.0
- FTP Programs

If you want to contact the editor of the magazine to get any help or advice re
sparkie@paragon.co.uk, or if you want to submit your homepage address to
webpages@paragon.co.uk

Link To: http://www.filemaker.com/

Adobe Page Mill – adding links

To make a link to another Web site, first highlight
the text where you want the link to be. Now, place
the cursor in the text bar at the bottom of the page
labelled 'Link to.' Enter the Web address and press
the return key to create the link. To create a link to
an email address, first highlight the object that you
want to link in. Now place the cursor into the 'link
to' box as before, but enter the prefix of 'mailto:'
before the email address itself. Press the return key
to create the link.

195

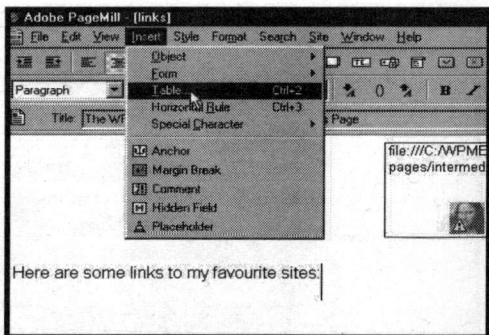

Adobe Page Mill – adding tables

To insert a table using PageMill, click on the 'Insert' menu and select 'Table' with the left mouse button. In the window which appears, you can set the number of rows and columns that you want to include in your table. Now that you've set up the skeletal structure of the table, you can add some content. To do this, place the cursor inside a cell and enter the content.

196

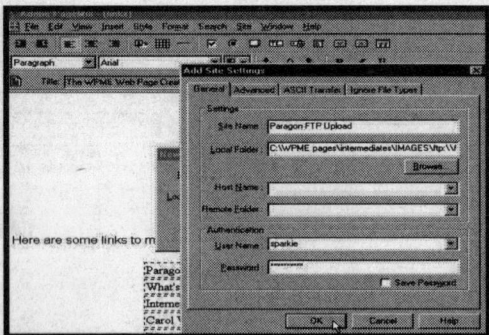

Adobe Page Mill – getting your site online

When you've saved your page to your hard drive, click on the 'File' menu and walk off the 'Upload' option. Once you have done this, you must select 'Page.' You're now asked to enter your FTP details – ask your ISP if you're unsure. Click on 'OK' once more to upload your page to the Web space server provided by your ISP.

197

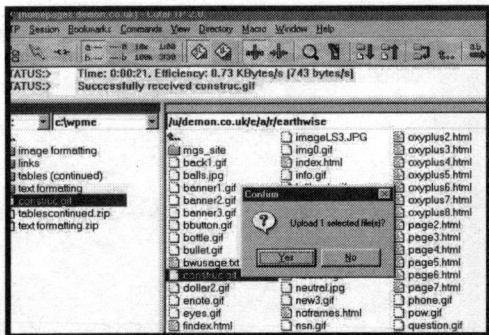

Easier file transfer

While you can get your site online ("uploading" it) using FrontPage Express or Composer, it's often easier to use a dedicated FTP program such as CuteFTP, which is on our CD. This is definitely the case if you have lots of files that make up your site. To transfer files with CuteFTP, you simply connect to your ISP and drag files from one side of the CuteFTP screen to the other.

198

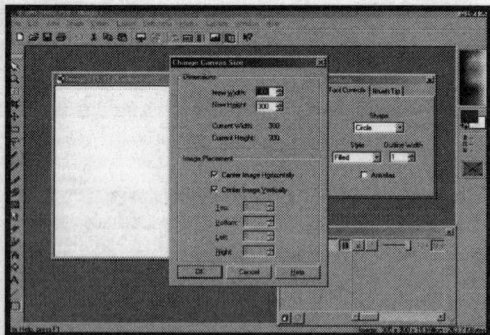

Edit images separately

You should prepare images for your Web site using an image-editing program such as Paint Shop Pro, on our CD. Try to keep images sizes as low as possible, under 35k if possible. Also, don't add too many images to your Web page or the download time will steadily increase. Net users have a short attention span, and will probably run out of patience.

199

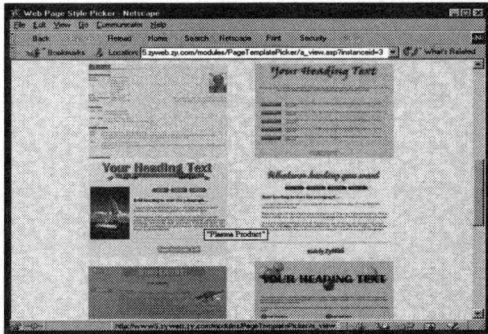

Get a customised Web site off the Web

If even the Web-site creation programs we have shown here seem too complicated, why not try ZyWeb? This is an easy to use online publishing solution – you simply connect to the Web site at http://www.zyweb.com and experiment with the free version. Follow the screens, adding your text and images, and a site will be created for you. See Web Pages Made Easy magazine for more guidance.

200

Get your site serviced

If you want to tune up your Web site, but don't know much about design, take a trip to http://www.websitegarage.com/. This site will check for any dead links throughout your site and even tell you how many people are linking to your Web site. You can even sign up for a regular newsletter about your site that points out the good and bad parts! Web Site Garage is particularly useful if you want to know how easy it is to find your site using search engines.

201

Is your website listed... use our free detective

did-it detective

The did-it.com detective utilizes our proprietary spider technology to check the search engines and directories to determine if your site has been indexed. This is the same monitoring technology our submission service uses to determine if site re-submission is necessary.

Please feel free to take advantage of a limited time offer and try the did-it.com detective for FREE. It will report back to you the current status your site has on the most popular engines.

ATTENTION DID-PLUS USERS: The detective service cannot be used to determine positioning of your site due to the enhanced nature of the did-it PLUS optimized pages we have created for you.

Please enter your URL:
http://

Locator Word or Phrase:

Type in the keyword phrase you want to use to test your findability.

We would like to send you additional information about did-it services and other information of interest to webmasters, site managers and interactive marketers. If you do not want to be part of these special mailings, please check here. Please view our **privacy** information. ☐

Registering sites with search engines

How do people find your Web site? Most find it by using search sites, or search engines. A good way of registering your site with search engines is to go one of the Web sites that offer this service. One of the best is Register-It, at http://www.register-it.com/free/. The free version will submit your site to the best 16 search engines on the Net. An alternative is Submit-It!, at http://siteowner.linkexchange.com/Free.cfm/. To check the status of your site submission to search engines, run a check through did-it detective, at http://www.did-it.com/.

GLOSSARY

There's an awful lot of Internet jargon to get your head around, as you've probably realised after spending an hour or two online. To help you sort your bauds out from your bandwidth and your ActiveX from your applets, we're printing a beginner-friendly glossary that explains all the most important jargon. This glossary is supplied by New Media in Business – to see an online version, complete with more detailed explanations, visit the Web site at http://www.nmib.com/.

ActiveX

A set of technologies that enables software components to interact with one another in a networked environment. It was developed by Microsoft and is currently administered as a Standard by the Open Group. In the context of the Internet, it is used for interactive components that add extra functionality to Web Sites, for a similar purpose to Applets.
See also: Applet.

AltaVista

One of the most popular search engines. The Web address is http://www.altavista.digital.com. See also: Search engines.
Anonymous FTP
Anonymous File Transfer Protocol. A mechanism for moving files from a user machine to, or from, a remote Internet machine anonymously. In other words, you do not have to identify yourself with a user name or password.
See also: FTP.

Applet

A small program that runs 'in a browser.' Applets are usually written in Java. They differ from applications in that they have restricted functionality that is designed to protect the users machine from faulty or malicious code. The restrictions include the inability to write to the user's hard disk, or execute operating system functions. The applets are downloaded from Web sites along with the Web page in which it was embedded. They are typically used to provide a more advanced user interface than HTML is capable of. See also: ActiveX, Java.

Archie

A system for finding files which are stored on
anonymous FTP sites.

ARPANET

Advanced Research Projects Agency Network and
the precursor to the Internet. It was created in 1969
by the US Department of Defence to conduct
research into networking.
See also: Internet.

Avatar

An image such as a human figure or face that users
choose to represent themselves in an online chat
forum.
See also: Chat Forum.

Backbone

A path through a network (such as the Internet)
that has a very high capacity. By taking a large part
of the network traffic over large distances, it helps
to speed up the network as a whole.
See also: Network.

Bandwidth

A measure of how much data can be transmitted down any connection. For example a normal telephone line with the latest modems has a bandwidth of 56,000 bits per second.

See also: Bps, Bit.

Baud

The baud rate of a modem is a measure of how many bits it can send or receive per second. Each baud is equal to 4 bits per second. So a 600 baud modem would process data at 2,400 bits per second.
See also: Bit, Modem.

Bit

The basic unit of storage in a computer. It can only hold two values a 0 or 1. All data stored in computers – numbers, letters, images, etc are made up on bits. Bit is derived from Binary Digit. A byte consists of 8 bits.
See also: Bps, Byte Bot.

Bps

Bits per second. A measurement of speed of data transfer from one place to another. For example, a 56,000bps modem can process 56,000 bits per second.

See also: Bandwidth, Bit.

Browser

A software tool which accesses Web sites, obtains
Web pages and displays them on the screen. It is
also used to support other Internet resources.
More details on this subject are available in the
online version of the HyperGlossary
(http://www.hyperglossary.co.uk).

Byte

The standard unit of measure for computer storage.
It is the unit that holds a single character (in
Western Alphabets) such as the letter 'A' or the
dollar sign '$.' Languages such as Chinese and
Japanese use two or more bytes for each character.
Each byte consists of 8 bits to represent the
character and one or more bits for internal
computer purposes.

   See also: Bit, Kilobyte, Megabyte, Gigabyte,
Terabyte.

Cache

In the context of the Web, the term is used to refer
to an area on a computer's disk that is used to store
files (Web pages, images, etc) that have been
downloaded from a Web site for you to view in your
browser. The files are stored so that if you want to
view the pages or images later, they can be
presented far more quickly – without waiting for
them to be downloaded a second time.

Cascading Style Sheets (CSS)
A mechanism for specifying the style of a Web page
separately from the Web page. The benefit is that
the look and feel of a set of Web pages can be
amended by altering one file that contains the style
rather than having to edit each of the Web pages.

Certificate

A document that is used to certify that a user or organisation are who they say they are. They contain information about who it belongs to, who it was issued by, expiry date and information that can be used to check out the contents of the certificate. It is as an important part of the SSL system for establishing secure connections.
See also: Certificate Authority, SSL.

Certificate Authority

An authority that issues certificates needed to authenticate users or organisations on the Internet.
See also: Certificate, SSL.

CGI

Common Gateway Interface. A set of rules for how programs can communicate with Web Server software. Programs that run on a Web Server and use the common gateway interface are called CGI programs.

CGI programs are written to process data that the Web user types into a form on a Web Page. They send results back to the user by generating a Web page and passing it to the Web Server software. CGI programs can be used to provide databases querying and updating facilities on Web sites.

Many Web Servers provide their own version of CGI. For example, ISAPI can be used with Microsoft Internet Information Server. It runs faster than CGI but will not work with all other web servers.
See also: Web Server.

Channel

A Web site that automatically downloads information to your computer according to a pre-arranged schedule.

This is also referred to as Push Technology.

Chat Forum

A group of Internet users exchanging messages on a subject of common interest. Unlike newsgroups, all the participants are connected to the forum at the same time and the messages are displayed immediately for members of the forum to see.

Client

A client machine is a computer that operates by obtaining some information or service from another machine – a server. For example your machine with a Web browser on is a client machine. To obtain Web pages, the browser goes to a Web server machine. The software that supports the operation of the client is known as client software.
See also: Server.

Client/Server

A client/server system is one where the users computer (the client) works with another computer (the server) in order to achieve the desired results. This contrasts with the traditional mainframes where everything is done on the mainframe with the (dumb) terminals simply displaying the results. The World Wide Web is a Client/Server system with the browser on the client computer requesting Web pages from the Web Server machine.

Cookie

A piece of information sent by a Web Server to a browser for storage on the client machine. The browser sends the information back to the Web Server when the latter requests it. This mechanism is used because the Web Server has no way of recognising a particular user when they revisit the site. In fact if you link from one page on the site to another on the same Web Site, the Web Server would not know that it is the same user looking at the two pages.

On sites that you log on to, cookies are used to hold your id and password (so you don't have to log on each page!) On shopping sites the cookie could be used to keep a list of what you have bought so far, so that you can choose things as you see them rather than having to restate what you want when you get to the checkout.

Crawler

A Web Crawler (or Spider) is a piece of software that scans the World Wide Web finding pages to add to the index of a search engine.
See also: Search Engines.

Directories

A World Wide Web directory is a Web Site that is used to locate Web sites and Web pages in predefined areas of interest. For each of these predefined areas, the directory provides a set of hypertext links to all the Web pages that fall within that area of interest.
More details on this subject are available in the online version of the HyperGlossary (http://www.hyperglossary.co.uk).

Discussion Group

An alternative name for the Newsgroups supported by Usenet.
See also: Usenet.

Domain Name

The domain name is the name that uniquely identifies organisations on the Internet. For example ual.com is the domain name of United Airlines, royal.gov.uk is the domain name of the British Royal family and my company is nmib.com. You will encounter them most frequently in Web addresses, mine is http://www.nmib.com/, and email addresses – mine is John@nmib.com.
See also: Email, URL.

Ecommerce

Electronic Commerce is conducting commerce over the Internet, such as buying products or services from Web sites.

Encryption

Encoding information before it is transmitted over the Internet so that no one else can read it except the computer that it is sent to.

Email

Electronic Mail is a mechanism for sending messages across a computer network. The text of the message is typed in on one computer and then is sent to someone else on the network. The recipient of the message reads it on his/her computer and can then delete the message, file it on the computer, print it, send a reply or forward it to other people on the network. Email is the standard abbreviation for Electronic Mail.

You can also use mailing lists to send a single message to many other users at the same time. More details on this subject are available in the online version of the HyperGlossary (http://www.hyperglossary.co.uk).

Extranet

An extranet is a private site which is accessed by a limited group of users over the Internet. Access to Extranet sites is restricted by password or other means.

More details on this subject are available in the online version of the HyperGlossary (http://www.hyperglossary.co.uk).

E-zine

An electronic magazine – in other words a magazine on the Web.

FAQs

Frequently Asked Questions. A set of questions with associated answers which set out to shed light on a particular subject area.

Fire Wall

A computer system that is used to prevent users on the Internet from getting unauthorised access to a LAN.
See also: LAN.

Flame Mail

Electronic Mail of an angry and often abusive nature. Typically sent to an Internet user who breaks the rules of one of the newsgroups, for example, advertising when in a group that forbids it.

Freeware

Software that is available free of charge. If software is free of charge for a limited (trial) period it is called shareware.

FTP

File Transfer Protocol. A mechanism for moving files between two machines over the Internet. An FTP site is a collection of documents, software, etc. which Internet users can transfer to their computers using FTP. The term 'anonymous ftp' is used to refer to sites where no user id or password is needed to access the files. In other words, the users are anonymous. FTP is also commonly used to transfer Web pages from the Webmaster's machine to the Web Server.

More details on this subject are available in the online version of the HyperGlossary (http://www.hyperglossary.co.uk).

Fuzzy Logic

A technique for matching items that are similar. For example, if you are using a search engine to find pages containing references to Stephen Thomson using fuzzy logic, it might well return pages that contain Stephen Thompson, Steven Thomson and Steven Thompson as well.

GIF

Graphic Interchange Format. One of the two standard formats used for image files on the Internet. The other standard format is JPEG. GIF format is well suited to diagrams and human created pictures and diagrams. It is also possible to do simple animations with the Animated GIF format. See also: JPEG.

Gigabyte

1,000 Megabytes, that is 1,000,000,000 bytes. The purists will tell you that it is actually the binary equivalent, which is 1024 x 1024 x 1024!
See also: Byte, Kilobyte, Megabyte, Terabyte.

Gopher

A predecessor of the World Wide Web which has been eclipsed by the latter's arrival. It works by providing a menu of hyperlinks that you can select from. This often leads to another menu which you select from until you eventually reach the document you were seeking. It is still used widely in the academic world.
See also: WWW, Hypertext.

Helper Application

An application that is used to process a file format that the browser cannot handle. Typically used for multimedia files and animations. Since there is an overhead in calling helper applications, plugs-ins are used for the most commonly used formats. Plug-ins fulfil the same function as helper applications, but they are in effect made part of the browser itself.
See also: Plug-in.

Hit

A hit count is used as a measure of the popularity of a Web Page. One is added to the hit count every time anyone reads the page. Some pages publish their hit counts. The hit count for a Web Site is the sum of all the hit counts for each file that makes up the Web. This is used to measure the overall popularity of the Web Site and the load on the Web Server.

Home Page

A home page is the starting point for browsing a set of Web pages. Every Web Site has a home page that is designed to be the first page seen. It typically has links to the various parts of the Web Site. A Browser also has a home page – the one that is displayed automatically when you invoke the browser. The leading browsers let you choose your own home page. This means you can ensure that your starting point is your favourite search engine, directory or the home page of your own Web Site if you have one. The term is also used for a Web page created by an individual to say who they are and describe their interests, etc – e.g. Jane Smith's home page.

Host

A computer on a network. The term is sometimes used to refer to computers that offer services to other computers such as running a Web Service or a Database.

HTML

HyperText Markup Language. The language used to create Web pages. It consists of a set of tags which indicate what action the browser should take when loading and processing the page. For example, the horizontal rule <hr> causes a horizontal line to appear.

There are also HTML tags for incorporating graphics into the file and for defining hyperlinks.

HTTP

HyperText Transport Protocol. The language that Web Browsers use to communicate with Web servers. You will no doubt recognise HTTP as a part the address of Web sites.

See also: Protocol.

HyperGlossary

An invented term to describe the combination of definitions and concepts provided by New Media in Business Ltd (http://www.nmib.com).

Hyperlink

A hyperlink is part of a Web page that provides a link to another part of the World Wide Web. The words Link and Hypertext link are used interchangeably with hyperlink.

More details on this subject are available in the online version of the HyperGlossary (http://www.hyperglossary.co.uk).

Hypertext

Text that contains hyperlinks to other documents. In other words, when the text is displayed you can click on certain regions of the document and are taken to elsewhere in the document or to another document. This is the basis of the World Wide Web.
See also: Hyperlink.

Id

A string of characters that identifies you, typically your name or initials, used when you are logging on to a computer system.
See also: Logon/Login.

IETF

See: Internet Engineering Task Force.
Internet
The Internet (with a capital I) is a vast network of computers that straddles the world which is open for anyone to join. It hosts the World Wide Web and provides an email connection for countless organisations and individuals. "internet" (with a lower case i) is a network that consists of two or more networks liked together. So the Internet is the most significant example of an internet.

Internet Engineering Task

Force (IETF)
The body that is responsible for most of the Internet Standards.
More details on this subject are available in the online version of the HyperGlossary (http://www.hyperglossary.co.uk) under Standards

Internet Service Provider

An Internet service provider is an organisation that offers Internet services including connection to the Internet and Web site hosting. Internet Service Providers are invariably referred to as ISPs.

Intranet

A private network that employs Internet Technology.
Usually the network will be restricted to a single organisation. The prime Internet technology that distinguishes an Intranet from a normal local area network is the use of the Web.
More details on this subject are available in the online version of the HyperGlossary (http://www.hyperglossary.co.uk).
IP Number
Internet Protocol Number. A number that is used to uniquely identify every computer on the Internet. It takes the following form:
189.104.232.8
Whenever you type in a Web address, the equivalent IP address is looked up in a directory and it is the IP address that is used to locate the relevant computer.
More details on this subject are available in the online version of the HyperGlossary (http://www.hyperglossary.co.uk).

IRC

Internet Relay Chat. A well established mechanism for supporting chat forums. Public and private forums are supported.
See also: Chat Forums.

ISDN

Integrated Services Digital Network. A mechanism for using existing telephone lines to provide higher bandwidth communication. Unlike the normal use of telephone lines for transmitting data, there is no need for a modem. The data is transmitted digitally rather than being converted to analogue (and back to digital at the far end). This permits faster connections between computers and faster transmission.

ISP

An Internet service provider is an organisation that offers Internet services including connection to the Internet and Web site hosting. Internet service providers are invariably referred to as ISPs.
For more details on this subject, go along to the online version of the HyperGlossary (http://www.hyperglossary.
co.uk).

Glossary

Java

Java is a programming language that is used for writing programs that can be downloaded to your computer through the Internet and immediately run within your browser. These programs are called applets. Java is a portable language that runs on any computer supported by a piece of software called the Java Virtual Machine (JVM for short). The popular browsers have a JVM built in and thus are capable of running Java applets.
See also: Applet.

JavaScript

A language that is embedded in Web pages and is executed by the browser as it displays the page. It can be used to make the Web page more dynamic and to validate the data that is typed into forms. Not to be confused with Java – which is a different language.
See also: VBScript.

JPEG

The Joint Photographic Experts Group (JPEG) format is one of the two standard formats used for images on the Web. The other is GIF. The JPEG format is well suited for photographic images.
See also: GIF.

Key Word

A word you type into a search engine to indicate what pages you would like it to locate for you.

Kilobyte

A thousand bytes. The purists will tell you that it is actually the binary equivalent, which is 1024!
See also: Byte, Megabyte, Gigabyte, Terabyte.

LAN

Local Area Network. A computer network situated within a given locality, typically one building or one site.
See also: WAN.

Leased-line

A telephone line connection between two points that is rented for exclusive use by an organisation. The advantage over redialling each time is that you get a consistent quality of line and resulting higher speed of data communication. It is usually cheaper when the line is in use for a large percentage of the time.

Link

An abbreviation for Hyperlink.

Login/Logon

The process of entering into a computer system is referred to as logging in or logging on. These terms are used most frequently when you have to identify yourself to the computer system by specifying an id and password. The id is a string of characters that identifies you, typically your name or initials. The password is a string of characters that only you know. The password is used to stop other people masquerading as you.

See also: Id, Password.

Mailing List

A mechanism for sending copies of a single email note to more than one recipient. The copies can be made on the user's machine. Alternatively a single copy is send to a server on the Internet for copying and sending on to the list of recipients. There are thousands of mailing lists operated on the Internet on all imaginable topics.

More details on this subject are available in the online version of the HyperGlossary (http://www.hyperglossary.co.uk).

Megabyte

A million bytes. The purists will tell you that it is actually the binary equivalent, which is 1024 x 1024! See also: Byte, Kilobyte, Gigabyte.

MIME

Multipurpose Internet Mail Extensions. The standard used on the Internet for identifying different types of file. It was initially introduced for attaching files to Internet email messages, but is also used by Web servers to inform browsers what type of file they are sending. Examples of MIME types are 'text/html' for standard Web pages and image/jpeg for JPEG files. Recent browsers and email systems handle a large number of MIME types automatically.

Mirror Sites

A mirror site of a Web site is an exact copy of the original site. They are commonly used for Web and FTP sites when the original site cannot cope with the load that is being put on it. An added benefit can be that one of the mirror sites is more accessible to you and therefore provides faster access.

Modem

Modulator demodulator. A device that is used to transmit data between two computers over a normal telephone line. You have one modem at each end of the phone line. At the sending end the data is converted into an analogue signal so that the telephone system can handle it, and at the receiving end the analogue system is converted back to digital form so that the computer can handle it.

Netiquette

Net etiquette. A set of guidelines on how you should behave when you are communicating over the Internet.
Netizen
Net citizen. Those who spend much of their time on the Internet. Used in the same way as you would talk about the citizens of Paris, for example.

Netscape

The company that is responsible for one of the leading browsers – Navigator and many other Internet products. It was the success of the early version of Navigator that started the rapid growth of the World Wide Web.

Network

Two or more computers connected together so that from one computer you can access data or run software on another computer.

Network News

An alternative name for Usenet.

Newbie

A person who is new to the Internet.

Newsgroup

A discussion group on Usenet.

NNTP

Network News Transport Protocol. The protocol used to support the Usenet service on the Internet. See also: Protocol.

Node

Any single computer on a network. Sometimes also referred to as hosts.

Password

The password is a string of characters that only you know. The password is used to stop other people masquerading as you. Sometimes the computer will check that not only have you typed the correct password in but that each letter is also in the correct case (upper or lower). To be effective, a password needs to be a string of characters that no one else could guess. So your name, initials, initials in reverse order are not good passwords. Mixing case and adding characters other than letters of the alphabet will help. Something like AZ9%3cG would be quite secure, the only problem being that you have to be able to remember it. See also: Login.

Plug-in

A browser plug-in is a computer program that adds functionality to the browser. The plug-ins are used to handle file formats that the browser cannot handle itself. The plug-ins in effect become part of the browser, and are more efficient that helper applications.
See also: Helper Applications.

Point of Presence

A location where a you can connect to the Internet or other network, typically via the telephone system. So, if an Internet Service Provider offers a Point of Presence in London, you will be able to access the Internet by phoning London. Not to be confused with the other POP – post office protocol.

POP

Abbreviation for Point of Presence and for Post Office Protocol.
See also: Point of Presence, Post Office Protocol.

Portal

A Web site that sets out to provide a point of entry to the World Wide Web. Examples are Yahoo! and Netscape Netcenter. They provide a wide selection of services (such as free email) and links to the rest of the Web. Their goal is to become your browser home page – the page that appears automatically each time you load your browser, or when you click on the home button.

Post Office Protocol

One of the standard protocols used by your email software when accessing email from the Internet. If your Internet service provider only supports POP, then you will need email software that can handle that protocol. The version number is often tagged on the end. Thus, POP3 is version 3 of the post office protocol.

Posting

A message sent to a newsgroup.
See also: Usenet.

Protocol

A language used to communicate between two computer programs. It consists of a set of commands and the rules about how they are used. A major cause of the success of the Internet has been the widespread adoption of a number of protocols, such as HTTP for communicating with Web Servers, FTP, etc.

Push Technology

A mechanism for sending information to your browser from a Web site at prearranged intervals. You state what information you are interested in and how often you want it updated and the Web site transmits its contents to you accordingly. You do not have to go back and request the latest information. The same technology is referred to as Netcasting by Netscape and Channels by Microsoft.

Rendering

The process of displaying a Web page in the browser – displaying the text in the correct size, font and colour, displaying images, etc.

RFC

Request For Comments. RFCs are used to reach agreement on Internet standards. A document (RFC) presenting a proposal for a new standard is published for comments. After taking appropriate actions on the comments a new version of the RFC is published for more comments. At some stage it is agreed to go with a particular RFC and those responsible start implementing. Thus an RFC can be a proposal or an agreed standard. There are also RFCs which provide background information on a particular subject. All RFCs can be viewed on the Internet.

Robot

Used to refer to a piece of software that performs a function in the place of a human being. Specifically the search engine tools that surf the Internet looking for pages to add to the search index is sometimes called a robot. The abbreviations bot or Web bot are also used.

Router

A computer at a junction on the Internet that directs data towards its correct destination. They decide which link of the network to send the data based on the IP number of the destination computer.
See also: IP number.

Search Engine

A search engine is a software tool that helps users find Web pages that relate to one or more key words that they have typed in.
More details on this subject are available in the online version of the HyperGlossary (http://www.hyperglossary.co.uk).

Server

A computer that provides a service to other computers on the network. For example, a Web server obtains Web pages and other files as requested by a Web user, and sends them to the browser. The term server is also applied to software packages that provide a service – so you also have Web server software, for example. The machines that connect to the server and use the services it offers are known as Client machines.
See also: Client.

SGML

Standard Generalized Markup Language, the international standard for defining descriptions of the structure and content of different types of electronic document. HTML is an example of a description which is defined with SGML.

Shareware

Software packages that you can use free of charge
for a trial period. After the trial period, you are
asked to make a payment. Some packages operate
on trust others have logic built into them to stop
them working at the end of the trial period. A lot of
Internet software is available as shareware.

SMTP

Simple Mail Transport Protocol. The protocol used to
send electronic mail over the Internet.

Spam (or Spamming)

The email equivalent of junk mail. The term is used in
particular to describe the practice of sending the same
message to a number of different Usenet groups or
mailing lists. Some groups and mailing lists have rules
against spamming, and offenders can get bombarded
with flame mail.

An inappropriate attempt to use a mailing list, or
USENET or other networked communications facility
as if it was a broadcast medium (which it is not) by
sending the same message to a large number of
people who didn't ask for it. The term probably comes
from a famous Monty Python skit which featured the
word spam repeated over and over. The term may also
have come from someone's low opinion of the food
product with the same name, which is generally
perceived as a generic content-free waste of
resources. (Spam is a registered trademark of Hormel
Corporation, for its processed meat product.)

For example, Mary spammed 50 USENET groups by
posting the same message to each.

See also: Maillist, USENET.

Spider

A Spider (or Web Crawler) is a piece of software that scans the World Wide Web finding pages to add to the index of a search engine.
See also: Search Engines.

SSL

Secure Sockets Layer. A protocol that supports secure communication over the Internet. SSL supports authentication and encryption. Authentication provides via certificates a means for you to validate who you are in contact with. Encryption codes all the data before it is transmitted, making it impossible for anyone else on the Internet to intercept and read your communications. This is important for shopping on the Web. It allows you check that the Web site is in fact owned by Dell Computers, and you can send your credit card details without fear that someone else on the Internet will see them.
See also: Certificate.

TCP

Part of the TCP/IP suite of protocols used to communicate between machines on the Internet. On the sending computer, TCP splits the data up into manageable sized packets and attaches information such as the IP number of the target computer. At the receiving computer, it checks all the packets have arrived and issues a request to resend a packet if necessary. When they have all arrived it extracts the data from each packet and assembles it in the correct sequence.
See also: TCP/IP, IP Number.

TCP/IP

Transmission Control Protocol/Internet Protocol. A set of protocols that are used by computers on the Internet to communicate with each other. It is used by all computers on the Internet or any Intranet. More details on this subject are available in the online version of the HyperGlossary (http://www. hyperglossary.co.uk).

Telnet

An Internet service that allows you to log into a remote computer.

Terabyte

1,000 gigabytes. The purists will tell you that it is actually the binary equivalent which is 1024 x 1024 x 1024 x 1024!
See also: Byte, Kilobyte, Megabyte, Gigabyte UDP.

URL

Uniform Resource Locator. The mechanism for addressing resources on the Internet. Uniform Resource Locator is invariably abbreviated to URL. The URL is best known for specifying Web addresses. For example, the URL for the New Media in Business Ltd glossary is http://www.nmib.com/ glossary/index.htm. This is what you type into the address field in the browser.
More details on this subject are available in the online version of the HyperGlossary (http://www.hyperglossary.co.uk).

User Datagram Protocol

One of the protocols for data transfer that is part of
the TCP/IP suite of protocols. Unlike TCP, UDP does
not check that all the data has been delivered. It is,
for example, used for conversations over the
Internet where:
1 The human brain will cope with a certain amount
of loss of speech.
2 By the time it discovers that some data is lost it
will be too late, and
3 The listener will ask the speaker to repeat if he she
doesn't understand.
See also: TCP/IP.

Usenet

An Internet service that provides support for
newsgroups (or discussion groups) on a large variety
of subjects. Each newsgroup consists of a collection
of electronic mail messages on a particular subject.
See also: Discussion Group Newsgroup.

Vaporware/Vapourware

Software products that do not really exist in a
usable form. The term was created as a result of the
fact that some software c

Directory Enquiries
http://www.bt.com/phonenetuk/

Postcodes
www.royalmail.co.uk/paf
www.scoot.co.uk
www.people.scoot.uk/